LIFE IN A
LIFELESS WORLD

Encountering Jesus in the Book of Hebrews

MICHAEL KIBBE

ivp
Academic
An imprint of InterVarsity Press
Downers Grove, Illinois

InterVarsity Press
P.O. Box 1400 | Downers Grove, IL 60515-1426
ivpress.com | email@ivpress.com

InterVarsity Press® is the publishing division of InterVarsity Christian Fellowship/USA®. For more information, visit intervarsity.org.

All Scripture quotations, unless otherwise indicated, are translated by the author.

While any stories in this book are true, some names and identifying information may have been changed to protect the privacy of individuals.

Interior images:
© Pramote Polyamate / Moment via Getty Images (rubble)
© enjoynz / DigitalVision Vectors via Getty Images (tree)

The publisher cannot verify the accuracy or functionality of website URLs used in this book beyond the date of publication.

Cover design: Faceout Studio, Jeff Miller
Interior design: Jeanna Wiggins
Images: Getty Images: © enjoynz / Moment; © sakchai vongsasiripat / Moment;
          © Pramote Polyamate / Moment

ISBN 978-1-5140-1026-6 (print) | ISBN 978-1-5140-1027-3 (digital)

Printed in the United States of America ∞

Library of Congress Cataloging-in-Publication Data
A catalog record for this book is available from the Library of Congress.

30 29 28 27 26 25 | 13 12 11 10 9 8 7 6 5 4 3 2 1

"In a world that often feels inhospitable to the life of faith, Michael Kibbe reminds us of the beauties of Jesus, who has passed through suffering into glory and who bids us to come and follow him. Discover afresh the wonders of the book of Hebrews and how Jesus' faithfulness is the fuel of our faithfulness and abundant life."

Philip Miller, senior pastor of The Moody Church

"How to survive in a world ill-equipped for sustaining life? Michael Kibbe draws on the condition of ectopic pregnancy—life in a space that cannot sustain it—as a window into the lessons taught in the book of Hebrews. Kibbe offers academic prowess, down-home practicality, conversational style, and splashes of real-life sorrow as he brings Hebrews alive. This fresh reframing of Hebrews will bear fruit in readers wherever they are in their journey with Christ through the wilderness we call life."

Lynn H. Cohick, distinguished professor of New Testament at Houston Theological Seminary

"From the heart of a scholar who has lived in Hebrews and the heart of a pastor who has lived the ups and downs of life, Michael Kibbe, in *Life in a Lifeless World*, offers readers an in-depth look at Hebrews to answer the real questions of those who want to have faith in the midst of a broken world. I cannot wait to put this into the hands of those who are interested in studying Hebrews, and even more, those who need to encounter the life-giving heart of God."

Amy Peeler, Kenneth T. Wessner Chair of Biblical Studies at Wheaton College and author of *Women and the Gender of God* and *Hebrews: Commentary for Christian Formation*

TO MY WIFE, ANNIE,

a conduit of love and life if ever there was one.

CONTENTS

ACKNOWLEDGMENTS

I'VE LOVED HEBREWS for as long as I can remember. I have feasted at its table my entire career, and done so in the company of many friends. Among those scholars who have wined and dined with me there are especially Ben Ribbens, Douglas Moo, Amy Peeler, David Moffitt, George Guthrie, Bobby Jamieson, Madison Pierce, Bryan Dyer, Jon Laansma, Jason Whitlark, Felix Cortez, and Gary Cockerill. I hope that this book represents them well even when it says things differently than they have.

Numerous individuals read this book, or significant portions thereof, long before it found a home with InterVarsity Press; I am especially grateful to Jenny Kaluza, John Mills, Kaleb Barkman, and Philip Miller. And as is often the case with books written by teachers, the first twenty drafts came out of the classroom rather than paper, so my gratitude is due to the students of Ecola Bible College and Great Northern University for their insights.

I will always think of the founders of Great Northern University when I seek modern participants in the hall of faith. Faculty, staff, administration, trustees, students, volunteers, and supporters—you saw what was then invisible, and you helped my unbelief.

I've been blessed to partner with IVP Academic on a number of projects over the years, and I am continually amazed by the caliber of people on that team. To Rachel Hastings in particular: the wounds of an editor are faithful!

This book has belonged to my wife, Annie, from the very beginning, as you will see if you keep reading. In sickness and in health, in fullness and in emptiness, in joy and in sorrow, God keeps us alive together, and together we invite you to share our story and share our life.

INTRODUCTION

STARBUCKS, DOWNTOWN SPOKANE, waiting for an appointment at the nearby Apple Store. Is there anything more generically twenty-first-century suburban American than that? I wish it hadn't happened there, but it did. I was getting ready to teach a portion of my systematic theology course at Great Northern University. My first year of teaching that course, my first year of working at that university. John Webster, in his book *Holy Scripture*, is taking me to school. A word jumps off the page, a word he did not intend to have the effect on me that it did. *Ectopic*. It comes from a Greek word that means "out of [*ek*] place [*topos*]." The church, says Webster, is "ectopic" because it exists in an environment from which it cannot receive its life.[1]

Webster is talking about the church, but in that moment I'm not thinking about the church. I'm thinking about the first time I heard the term *ectopic*, and it wasn't in a theology textbook. It was spoken by an OB-GYN as she rushed my wife and me out the door, into our van, and toward the hospital. Annie had been experiencing some miscarriage symptoms, and the pregnancy tests couldn't make up their mind—were we expecting our second child or not? We showed up at the doctor's office at 1:00 p.m., we arrived back home at our apartment at 7:30 p.m., and in between were the most surreal six and a half hours of our lives.

An ectopic pregnancy typically occurs when the fertilized egg implants itself in a fallopian tube rather than in the uterus (thus the alternate name *tubal* pregnancy). It's "out of place." That's a problem, because it can't survive—fallopian tubes are not equipped for nine-month residency.

---

[1]John B. Webster, *Holy Scripture: A Dogmatic Sketch* (Cambridge: Cambridge University Press, 2003), 47.

Sometimes the mother's body recognizes the problem and miscarries. Sometimes it doesn't, and the baby manages to grow a little bit from the sparsely available nutrients. And that growth is deadly, because sooner or later, the fallopian tube will rupture, and the mother will bleed out internally. Apart from advanced medical technology, such as ultrasounds and surgery centers, it's a death sentence for the mom and for the baby.

"You need to go to the hospital." "Can we stop by our apartment and—?" "No. Go to the hospital *now*." Two hours later I'm sitting in the hospital waiting room, surrounded by friends, trying to keep it together until the digital screen on the wall switches from "Kibbe–In Operating Room" to "Kibbe–In Recovery." By dinnertime I am helping Annie walk gingerly up the stairs to our apartment, where Sean, our one-year old, is sitting on the floor with some good friends, eating Cheerios and having not a clue in the world.

We barely had time that day to take a breath. But when we did, we had questions. Some logistical—how do we care for a toddler whom Mommy can't pick up for six weeks? Some personal—will we ever get pregnant again? And, of course, the big one: What exactly just happened? Three of us entered that hospital, and only two came out. The surgeon saved Annie's life by removing what he afterward called "ectopic tissue." *Tissue.* That's our *child* you're talking about. We're not angry at him—did I mention he saved Annie's life and that he did so in the only way known to humanity at this stage of medical development? We're hardly second-guessing the decision, but we still have questions.

We figured out the logistics, as so many families have in such circumstances. We did get pregnant again—our daughter's name is Eliana, which means "my God answers." We grieved and processed, with each other and with our community, the best we knew how. And we moved on together—until seeing the word *ectopic* in Webster's book years later brought it all back.

It could have been a news headline, or a friend recounting their own story, or some other random experience. Any spark might have lit this flame. But God chose to use a technical book by a British theologian who wasn't talking about pregnancy at all, and God did that, I think, because he wanted to lead me into another phase of this journey, starting with the recognition that Webster was on to something. The church is ectopic. It is out of place. It cannot receive its life from its location. But what does that mean, exactly? And if our life does not come from our immediate environment, from where does it come? How? And why? And who cares? What no surgeon could do for our baby, God does for us. God sustains our life, collectively and individually, within an environment that is incapable of doing so by itself. This book is about how he does this, and why, and what difference it ought to make to my misplaced existence (quite a lot, as it turns out). And I don't mind telling you that there might be some surprises along the way. The first surprise is where we go for answers to these questions. There is in the New Testament a book we call Hebrews. Hebrews was written to God's people in their struggle to remain alive despite existing in an environment that could not provide that life—like a fetus in a fallopian tube, they needed sustenance from without. And Hebrews showed them—and shows us—how God provides that life, sustains that life, and invites us to put that life on display.

The second surprise comes in how, according to Hebrews, God has accomplished all this. If you've read Hebrews, or even if you haven't, you might guess that the answer has something to do with *Jesus*. So try this on for size: Jesus, by virtue of his resurrected human life and priestly position at the right hand of the Father in heaven, sustains the lives of his brothers and sisters on earth until the day that he brings them into his universal inheritance and kingship over all of God's creation. And in the meantime he invites us to live that life through faith, hospitality, sexual fidelity, generosity, and suffering.

You might also be surprised, as I was years ago, at how common ectopic pregnancies are. The medical literature estimates, based on reported diagnosed cases in US hospitals, that 1-2 percent of pregnancies in this country are ectopic.[2] Given that between 3.5 and 4 million babies

---

[2]As reported by the National Library of Medicine. See Erin Hendriks, Rachel Rosenberg, and Linda Prine, "Ectopic Pregnancy: Diagnosis and Management," *American Family Physician* 101, no. 10 (May 2020): 599-606, https://pubmed.ncbi.nlm.nih.gov/32412215/.

are born in the United States each year, that's an astounding number of ectopic pregnancies in this country alone.[3] But ectopicness comes in different forms. Being out of place and failing to find life in one's current situation—that's not a 1-2 percent occurrence. More like 100 percent. Who *hasn't* experienced that? The teenager who went home in March 2020 for Covid lockdown and emerged two years later with nothing to show for it but gaming expertise and profound loneliness. *I interact with people online all the time—why do I feel like no one really knows me?* The middle-aged couple wondering whether they'll bother staying together as empty nesters. *I just don't know if we're headed the same direction.* The millennial waking up to the feeling that they've been sold a bill of goods on the American dream. *I thought I was going to change the world.* The young single coming to the city for a first career opportunity, along with the widow slowly fading away in a rundown apartment. *How can I be known when everyone who knows me is somewhere else?* The young mom whose personhood has disappeared beneath a pile of diaper bags and Pack 'n Plays. *Is this all that there is to me?* The midcareer professional sitting at a Starbucks waiting for his Genius Bar appointment—the irony of being confronted with my own ectopicness in that particular space is quite something. *The best and brightest of modern American marketing told me this was precisely the kind of person I wanted to be.*

We're all ectopic. We're all living in a place that can't sustain us. So the real question is, What are we going to do about it? Option A is to believe the hype, believe the lies, about substances or behaviors or relationships or possessions or positions or experiences that are presented as sources of meaning, fulfillment, sustenance, *life*. And to pursue life where it may not be found is to pursue death—every ounce of energy and every drop of sweat given to pulling that bucket out of the empty well is simply taking us closer to our inevitable demise. Is it really surprising, given how quick we are to follow these paths to nowhere, that addictions are skyrocketing and mental health is in free fall?

---

[3]As reported by the CDC. See "Births and Natality," CDC, last reviewed September 27, 2024, www.cdc.gov/nchs/fastats/births.htm.

Option B is to seek life where it may be found. That, ultimately, is what this book is all about. But notice, right here at the beginning of our journey together, that option B is not to *leave* the place we are in. God has led us to the wilderness. God has called us to *live ectopically*, not to *escape ectopicness*. So this book isn't about leaving the world. "This world is not my home, I'm just a-passing through"—nope. Wrong. This world is our home, but at the moment, this world can't sustain us. The question isn't how to get out of the world but how to continue to be in the world and yet receive life from beyond it *and* be a conduit of life to it until that day when God renews the world and it becomes a place of life for us once again.

I don't mind telling you that there's some heavy lifting on the interpreting-the-Bible front in this book—Hebrews is dense; there's just no way around that. So I'm going to do my best to lead you through some deep waters without either of us drowning. We'll start with a little warmup on what Hebrews is, where it came from, and what sorts of questions might be the right ones to keep us on track. And on occasion, throughout the book, I'll stop and say something like, "I know this raises some complicated questions, but in order to stay focused I'm going to keep moving forward and put some additional—and slightly more technical—discussion of this point at the end of the book." So at the end of the book there are a handful of "Going Deeper" sections for those so inclined.

The first major part of the book addresses Jesus' own life, especially as it is portrayed in Hebrews 1–2. These chapters show us his journey from in place to out of place to in a better place. In particular, they show us that the two most important moments in Jesus' story were his atonement (when he solved the sin problem and made it possible for us to receive life from God) and his enthronement (when he sat down at his Father's right hand in heaven and offered us the chance to share in his life from there).

The second part focuses on Jesus' provision of life. Here we learn exactly what atonement is all about and how Jesus giving his life to his Father is what makes it possible for God the Father to give that life to us. If you've grown up in church and spent any significant amount of time reading the Bible, you might think this is the easy part—"Jesus died for my sins so I could have eternal life," or something of that sort. Well, you're certainly not wrong that Jesus died so that you could live. But there's a *lot* more going on than that.

The third part addresses Jesus' invitation into life. There's a birthday present sitting on the dining room table, metaphorically speaking. But, as it turns out, God's not a long-distance giver. You want something from God? You have to be *with* him. Because of Jesus, we have a foot in two worlds, so to speak—like Israel in the wilderness, we are journeying toward the place God is preparing for us, but even in our wilderness God is there with us and sustaining us. To be alive is to be with God. That's the only way. And, once again like Israel in the wilderness, being with God and receiving life from God is quite the serious undertaking. "Our God is a consuming fire," says Hebrews 12:29, so the first part of the invitation is to get *real* close, but the second part is to not be foolish in doing so.

The fourth part concerns putting Jesus' life (in us) on display. To be ectopic is to die—so how, exactly, does one *live* ectopically? Well, Hebrews says it starts with *faith*. Faith that what is right in front of us cannot sustain us, faith that something else can. Faith to persevere. Faith to reject false promises of life, faith to endure death because even death cannot cut off the life supply that we have from elsewhere.

Hebrews also says that ectopic living, life in a lifeless world, living as though "here we have no lasting city" (Heb 13:14), means *love*. Love manifested as hospitality and generosity, because with an unrelenting source of life outside myself, I can afford to share what I have with others. Love embodied in suffering, because what the world can't sustain, it inevitably rejects. Love displayed in all sorts of ways as the life of Christ overflows abundantly into us, and abundantly out from us into the very world that needs from us what it cannot give to us.

SECTION 1

JESUS' OWN LIFE

WE NATURALLY GRAVITATE toward portions of the Bible that feel familiar. Stories we have heard since childhood—Noah and the flood, David and Goliath, Jesus healing a leper or calming a storm. Short proverbs with easily applied wisdom for the day. Songs that put words to our deepest feelings of abandonment, joy, anger, or thankfulness. Letters with clear introductions that help us settle in—"I, Paul . . . to the church in [Ephesus/Corinth/Rome]." But there are other parts of the Bible that start strange and stay that way, no matter how long we stare at them. Genealogies full of names we can barely pronounce, laws about sacrifices we'll never offer, endless diatribes against this or that evil nation. Most of the rough ground is in the Old Testament, but if there is a "None of this makes sense, and I'm not even sure where to begin, so I think I'll try something else" part of the New Testament, it's probably the book we call Hebrews. Revelation is weirder, to be sure, but stories about dragons with seven heads and beasts with ten horns are at least fascinating, even if we have no idea what it all means. Hebrews, on the other hand, is just *hard*. Hebrews 11 is nice: a whole bunch of people had faith, and God rewarded them for it. And the general idea seems to be something like "Jesus is awesome," so that has some potential. But sacrifices and altars and covenants and priests and dire warnings about falling away and God being a consuming fire and one quote after another from the Old Testament that doesn't get explained— it's all a bit much. And on top of all that, there is nothing at the beginning to get us situated; in fact, many scholars have suggested that the first sentence of Hebrews is the most densely packed and challenging sentence in the entire New Testament.[1] So how do we even get started?

If you've ever been taught how to study the Bible, whether in an academic setting, or at church, or in a small group or anywhere else, you've probably been told that the original context—meaning, the historical setting within which a particular part of the Bible was written and read—is vitally important. I wholeheartedly affirm that principle, but we need to recognize before getting underway that Hebrews has long frustrated those who want to study the Bible in its original context, because we know almost nothing about Hebrews' original context. The fact is, we don't know any of the key pieces of information: *who* wrote it, *to whom*, *where* it was written, *when* it was written, or even *why* it was written. There are many theories, of course, but we're still waiting for one that is substantiated by the available evidence and really helps us understand Hebrews.

Here are some things we *don't* know that are often presented as part of the background of Hebrews. First, if you've heard a sermon or sermon series on Hebrews, you may have heard that the audience was thinking about leaving Jesus and going back to Judaism. But Hebrews doesn't say this. It does compare Jesus to various Old Testament practices and realities, and it does suggest that Jesus is superior to them, but there are plenty of reasons why the author might have done that other than to convince people not to go back to those things.[2] Second, you might also have heard, particularly with reference to Hebrews 1, that the audience had some weird ideas about angels—that they were equal with Jesus, or maybe even superior to Jesus. Again: Hebrews doesn't say this. It does compare Jesus to angels, but there are many reasons why the author might have done this other than to combat a particular brand of bad angelology.[3]

---

[1]David A. Black, "Hebrews 1:1-4: A Study in Discourse Analysis," *Westminster Theological Journal* 49 (1987): 175-76; John P. Meier, "Structure and Theology in Heb 1,1-14," *Biblica* 66 (1985): 170.

[2]Sigurd Grindheim, *The Letter to the Hebrews*, Pillar New Testament Commentary (Grand Rapids, MI: Eerdmans, 2023), 32.

[3]If you preach or teach, starting your series with what amounts to "This book isn't relevant to you because it was written to address problems you'll never have" might not be the best way to get your audience fired up. How many people in your audience worship angels?

Here's what we *do* know: Hebrews was written sometime in the mid-to late first century AD by a second-generation follower of Jesus—meaning, he wasn't one of the apostles who was taught by Jesus himself; he heard about Jesus from the apostles (Heb 2:3).[4] He was very well educated, both in terms of his writing style and his deep knowledge of the Old Testament. We also know that the recipients of the book were people who had been following Jesus for some time but were slacking off for some reason (Heb 5:11-12), that they had experienced persecution in the past (Heb 10:32-34), and that there were some people with the author and known to the audience who were from Italy (Heb 13:24). That's pretty much it. Historical background is a "do what you can with what you have" component of biblical interpretation: if you've got a lot of information, as we frequently do with Paul's letters, for example, use it; if you haven't got a lot of information, as is the case with Hebrews, don't lose any sleep over it. Do what you can with what you have, and in this instance, we don't have much.

That's the good news: you're not going to need to become an expert historian to read Hebrews reasonably well. Of course, the fact that Hebrews doesn't identify its own precise historical moment doesn't mean it didn't have one. It was written in the first century AD, in Greek, by a person solidly educated in both the Old Testament and the philosophies of his day, probably to an audience about whom we could say the same.[5] It was written from somewhere in the Roman Empire to somewhere else in the Roman Empire. It was written to people who were struggling to find life in their ongoing pursuit of Jesus, for a variety of reasons, which is why Hebrews speaks so well to our similar struggles today. All these things need to be taken into consideration when reading Hebrews, if for

---

How many are thinking about ditching Christianity and converting to (non-Messianic) Judaism?

[4]Amy L. B. Peeler, *Hebrews*, Commentaries for Christian Formation (Grand Rapids, MI: Eerdmans, 2024), 17.

[5]Of the many studies of Hebrews concerned with its historical context, the recent works of Michael Martin and Jason Whitlark on the use of ancient rhetorical devices in Hebrews have proven the most helpful. See especially Michael W. Martin and Jason A. Whitlark, *Inventing Hebrews: Design and Purpose in Ancient Rhetoric*, Society for New Testament Studies Monograph Series 171 (Cambridge: Cambridge University Press, 2018).

no other reason than to keep us from assuming that the original situation of Hebrews was the United States in the twenty-first century. But the kind of specific connections we can frequently make between Paul's letters and their historical context (meals in Corinth, citizenship in Philippi) elude us here, so we must be far more cautious in using historical connections to determine the meaning of any given text in Hebrews.

On the other hand, and you've probably picked up on this if you've read Hebrews in the past, the author is clearly familiar with the Old Testament and expects the same from his readers. If you want to do the background work to get ready to dive into Hebrews, your best bet is to spend some time in the Old Testament. The fact is, you've got as much chance of grasping Hebrews without carefully studying the Old Testament as of winning the Stanley Cup without a goalie. But that doesn't mean you need to put Hebrews away until you've read the Old Testament and understood everything in it. One of the major goals of this book is to get you properly oriented to how Hebrews is reading the Old Testament, and Hebrews can teach *you* to read it as well. If you're suddenly feeling a bit behind on your Old Testament trivia, relax—we'll get there. And, truth be told, if you're feeling a bit intimidated by Hebrews, whether because of all the Old Testament references in it or for some other reason, well, there's no avoiding it: some things in Hebrews are difficult to understand. Melchizedek, tabernacles in heaven, recrucifying Jesus—these are not your run-of-the-mill small group discussion topics.

For what it's worth, at least some of these topics were quite challenging to the original audience as well, but that didn't prevent the author from writing about them anyways (Heb 5:11-14). Apparently, the potential benefits of growing in their commitment to following Jesus were worth wrestling with some things that would be overwhelming at first glance. So get ready, because some of this is going to be more like hiking up the mountain through deep snow drifts with the wind in your face than the downhill, soft-powder ski run that we sometimes expect studying the Bible to be. But remember two things as you do so. First, the beauty of the view from the top is usually proportionate to the number of calories you burn on the way there. Second, there is someone up ahead, waiting for you, cheering you on, reminding you that not only did *he* persevere to the triumphant and glorious end for which God created you, but he has made it possible for you to do likewise.

1

JESUS ON HIS THRONE

IT'S A FAMILIAR LITERARY TROPE: a character or set of characters, living their mundane lives, is exposed to a world of which they had not previously been aware. Lucy Pevensie discovers Narnia, Neo escapes the Matrix, you know the drill. Sometimes such stories reveal to the protagonist that their old world is entirely fraudulent, but other times they invite that character to return to their old world but live differently in it.

This second strategy is often going on not only within these stories themselves but within the experience of reading them. We, the protagonists in the event of reading, are drawn into new worlds created by our favorite authors. Eventually we have to put the book down—we have to go to work, converse with a friend, go to bed, make a meal, play a game with our kids, whatever. We leave that literary world and go back to our tangible world, but, if the book is any good, something of it will go with us, and we will live in our old worlds differently because of our participation in that new world.

The Bible offers this readerly experience: when I sit down at my desk and read Hebrews, I lose myself in a world where God the Father speaks to God the Son in heaven in the presence of many angels, where character after character defies death and lives by faith, where bones lie in the desert as testimony to God's faithfulness to his promise despite his people's unfaithfulness to theirs. And as a reader I am invited to get up from my desk and go back to my life but live differently in this world because of my time in that one.

The Bible also identifies us as the protagonists in the story itself, because it presents itself as *real*. Middle-earth exists in the mind of J. R. R. Tolkien and in the minds of millions of readers, but it doesn't exist in the sense that I might meet an elf or battle an orc, or in the sense that I could go to Hobbiton or Gondor. But when Hebrews says that the Son sits enthroned in heaven, it means it. Wherever (whatever?) heaven is, Jesus—a real, live, flesh-and-blood human being—is there.

Reading Hebrews 1 should make us uncomfortable. It should disorient us, because by showing us a world where things are as they should be, it also tells us that our world is not as it should be. Does *your* world reflect the absolute supremacy of God's Son, Jesus? When you look around, do you think, *Wow, God has spoken, and my world is obviously listening to him speak and submitting to his words?* I sure don't. I emerge from the world of Hebrews 1 and look at the world in which I live, and I think, *Something's wrong. My world is a mess. Satisfaction and fulfillment and meaning and life are not available here in the way they ought to be.* "Do you feel the world is broken? We do."[1] If we didn't, we wouldn't be killing ourselves trying to fix it. If this world could give me life, I wouldn't be looking so hard to find it elsewhere.

But while we sit here in our world, rightly singing songs of brokenness and shadows, the angels depart the throne room of God singing a different tune. *The Son sits. The king reigns. All things will belong to him, and we are sent to serve those whose inheritance is as certain as his. Jesus is coming.* Life *is coming.* He hasn't yet, and so I feel out of place, and I should feel out of place, because like the rich man in Jesus' parable, I can see across the chasm to where life is as it should be, and I'm not there. Yet.

God Spoke (Hebrews 1:1-4)

The first sentence of Hebrews is a monster:

> God, after speaking in the past in many different ways to the fathers through the prophets, spoke in these last days to us through the Son, whom he appointed heir of all things, through whom he

---

[1] Andrew Peterson, "Is He Worthy?," *Resurrection Letters: Prologue*, Centricity Music, 2018.

made the ages, and who, being the radiance of his glory and the
exact representation of his being, and sustaining everything by his
powerful word, after accomplishing atonement for sins, sat down
at the right hand of the Majesty on high, and by doing so became
as much greater than the angels as the name that he has inherited
is superior to theirs. (Heb 1:1-4)

Yes, that's one sentence. But keep in mind: a sentence is nothing more
than a subject, a verb, and a whole bunch of trimmings. Find the subject
and the verb; ignore everything else for a moment. *God spoke.* That's it.
Or, if you want to add just one more component, you could say, *God,
after speaking, spoke.* Everything else is just window dressing to that
basic claim. So let's pause for a moment and reflect on what that tells us
about Hebrews. First, this whole book is going to be about things that
God spoke. Second, it's going to be about the fact that *God spoke* more
than once: first one way, then another. Third, before we start thinking
that Hebrews is about why Judaism is bad and the Old Testament is bad
(every time we say the former we end up thinking the latter, even if we
never actually say it) and Jesus is better than all that, we'd better notice
something: the most important thing Hebrews wants to say about the
Old Testament is that *God spoke* it. And that means, perhaps surpris-
ingly, that before Hebrews says anything about how old and new are
different, it's said something about how they are the *same.*[2]

Fourth and final point: there's a word missing from the sentence
above that might show up in your translation of the Bible: *but.* Some
English translations say "God spoke to the fathers . . . , *but* now he has
spoken to us." The word *but* (or, that is, its ancient Greek equivalent)
does not appear in the original text of Hebrews. It's not there, and it
shouldn't be in our translations either, because it implies that Hebrews
is setting up negative-positive comparison when it isn't. There's a world
of difference between "After speaking in the past, God spoke in the
present" and "God spoke in the past *but* now has spoken in the present."

[2]Gene R. Smillie, "Contrast or Continuity in Hebrews 1.1-2," *New Testament Studies* 51
(2005): 543-60.

The first draws our attention to what's the same in each case, while the second fixes our gaze on what's different.

Moving on. Every other part of this sentence answers questions about the basic claim that *God, after speaking, spoke.*

Q: *When* did he speak?

A: In the past and in these last days.

Q: *To whom* did he speak?

A: To the fathers and to us.

Q: *How* did he speak?

A: Through the prophets and through the Son.

Q: *What* did he say?

A: Oddly enough, there's no answer to this one. Hold that thought for later.

Notice, now, that the rest of the sentence is less about God speaking and more about the one through whom he spoke: the Son. It gets complicated, so try this:

The Son is

- the one God appointed heir of everything
- the one through whom God made everything
- the one who

  - *[being the radiance and the exact representation,*

  - *sustaining everything,*

  - *and after accomplishing atonement,]*

  sat down at God's right hand

  [and, as a result of sitting, became superior to the angels.]

Think of it this way. There are three things we need to know about the Son: he has been appointed heir, he was God's agent of creation, and he sat down. And the rest, once again, answers questions about the fact that he sat down.

Q: *Who*, exactly, is this Son who sat down?

A: He is the radiance of God's glory and the exact representation of his nature, and the one who sustains everything with his powerful word.

Q: *When* did he sit down?

A: After accomplishing atonement.

Q: *What resulted from* his sitting down?

A: He became as much superior to the angels as the name that he has inherited is superior to theirs.

There's a lot we could say about all this, but I'll stick to three particularly important issues. First, the two pivotal phrases about what Jesus did are that he "accomplished atonement for sins" and then "sat down at the right hand of the Majesty on high." From the second sentence of Hebrews to the very last, everything comes back to these two moments. How did Jesus accomplish atonement? Where and when did he accomplish atonement? When did he sit down, and what permitted him to do so? And, of course, why should we care? There's not one piece of Hebrews, from Hebrews 1:5 to Hebrews 13:21, that doesn't bring us back to these two moments in one way or another. After accomplishing atonement, he sat down (what we call his session or his enthronement). Atonement and enthronement. Keep those two events in mind.

The second thing I notice is that whoever this Son is, he's not like anyone else we've ever met in the pages of Scripture. He created everything, he keeps everything going, and he will inherit everything. He doesn't *reflect* God's glory, like a mirror reflects light; he is the light itself that makes the mirror's reflection possible. Or to put it in other biblical terms, he isn't "in" God's image, like you and I are; he *is* the image in which you and I are made.[3] He is what only God is; he does what only God does.

---

[3]Carmen Imes has recently proposed that Gen 1:26 should actually be translated, "Let us make humanity *as* our image." See Imes, *Being God's Image: Why Creation Still Matters* (Downers Grove, IL: IVP Academic, 2023), 4-6. Her point is not to minimize the distinction between us and Jesus but simply to ensure—and on this point she is undoubtedly correct—that being made in this manner "is essential to human identity rather than a

It was claims about the Son such as these found in Hebrews 1 that com-
pelled the early church to formulate the early creedal statements about
Jesus' deity, contrary to occasional suggestions today that the creeds are
what happens when biblical statements get forced into Greek philo-
sophical molds.[4] Even the critics recognize that we don't have to move
very far to get from the claims of Hebrews 1 to the claims of the creeds.

And yet—here's the third point. Many have suggested that Hebrews 1 is
about the Son being divine, while Hebrews 2 is about the Son being human,
but this hardly does justice to the remainder of our sentence, particularly
the final phrase, "he became as much superior to the angels as the name
that he has inherited is superior to theirs."[5] He *became* superior to the
angels. Meaning, there was a time at which he was *not* superior to the
angels. Say what? He created everything, presumably including the angels;
he radiates the glory of God, is exactly like God in his nature, and yet had
to *become* superior to the angels? If the purpose of Hebrews 1 is to say,
"Jesus is God, so he's superior to the angels," this is perhaps not the easiest
way to go about it. God didn't *become* superior to the angels. He just *is*. So
we move into the rest of Hebrews 1 and into Hebrews 2 with a question:
How can the Lord and Creator of angels *become* superior to those angels?

The Son Sat (Hebrews 1:5-14)

The rest of Hebrews 1 is a string of quotes from various parts of the Old
Testament, mostly the Psalms. Some of them are about the Son, some of

---

capacity that can be lost" (6). In other words, we are no less valuable in God's eyes (and
therefore in each other's eyes) by our divergence from acting out image bearing/being.

[4]This idea, termed the Hellenization (meaning, "Greek-ization") thesis, is certainly valid
insofar as Christian thinkers have at times become more conversant with the modes of
thinking that belong to their own cultural moment than the modes of thinking that belong to Scripture itself. But as a broad framework for naming what systematic theology
is in relation to the Bible, it fails miserably. See David S. Yeago, "The New Testament and
the Nicene Dogma: A Contribution to the Recovery of Theological Exegesis," *Pro Ecclesia*
3 (1994): 152-64, for a particularly helpful discussion of this issue.

[5]For classic essays putting the flow of Heb 1–2 in such terms, see Richard Bauckham, "The
Divinity of Jesus Christ in the Epistle to the Hebrews," in *The Epistle to the Hebrews and
Christian Theology*, ed. Richard Bauckham et al. (Grand Rapids, MI: Eerdmans, 2009),
15-36; John B. Webster, "One Who Is Son: Theological Reflections on the Exordium to
the Epistle to the Hebrews," in Bauckham et al., *Epistle to the Hebrews*, 69-94.

them are about angels, some are about both. But it's really easy to get caught up in the details of where a quote was taken from, whether it was taken out of context, which ancient version of the Bible the author of Hebrews was using, and so on, and miss the big picture. The big picture, as in the opening lines of Hebrews, is the simple subject-verb combination that tells us what the whole thing is about: *God spoke*. See the phrase near the beginning of Hebrews 1:5, 6, 7, 8, 10, 13: "God/he says." And the rest of each verse answers questions about that basic claim. So, let's ask some questions about God's speeches here, starting with this one: *When* did God say all these things?

Hebrews 1:5-14 hints at the timing of God's speech to the Son and the angels in three places. First, in the very first quote (Heb 1:5, taken from Ps 2:7), God says, "You are my Son; *today* I have become your Father." The previous verse points out that the Son became superior to the angels on account of his superior name, and the following verses suggest that the title *Son* is that name, so the story goes something like this: Jesus became superior to the angels when God identified him as Son in some particular way. And since we've already learned that he took on that name "after accomplishing atonement for sin," we can safely assume that the timeline, so far, goes like this: atonement → named Son → became superior to the angels.

The second hint comes at the end of the chapter: Which of the angels did God ever invite to sit at his right hand (Heb 1:13, taken from Ps 110:1)? We already know that the Son sat down after receiving the superior name, which happened after he accomplished atonement, so now the sequence goes like this: atonement → named Son → became superior to the angels → invited to sit down → sat down. Notice how the two key events from the first sentence (atonement and enthronement) bracket everything else. If the question is, "When did God say all these things in Hebrews 1:5-14?" the answer so far is, "After the Son accomplished atonement but before he sat down."

The third hint about the timing of all this might seem to contradict what I've said so far. Hebrews 1:6 says, "When he brings the firstborn into the world, God says. . . ." Undoubtedly, if you're familiar with the biblical story at all, you read "brings the firstborn into the world" and immediately thought, *Jesus' birth—Bethlehem—the incarnation*. But the previous two hints would seem to say, rather differently, that God said these things to Jesus after he had died, been raised, and ascended to heaven.

Here's the problem: the word that most English Bibles translate as "world" in Hebrews 1:6 doesn't mean "earth," as opposed to "heaven," which is what most of us think when we see that word. It actually describes some sort of inhabited space and, ironically, in this context refers to heaven.[6] The scene depicted so far in Hebrews 1 is of the Son ascending to heaven, having accomplished atonement but not yet having sat down, now standing before God and the inhabitants of heaven—the angels. In addition, if we skip forward a little bit, Hebrews 2 is going to say that in the incarnation, Jesus is going to become *lower* than the angels (Heb 2:9). But Hebrews 1:6 says that when God brings his firstborn Son into "the world," he says, "Let all God's angels worship him!" If Jesus' birth involves his becoming *lower* than the angels, it doesn't fit too well into our current context (in Heb 1) of Jesus becoming so much *higher* than the angels that God commands them to worship him.[7]

Keeping in mind that God says all these words in Hebrews 1:5-14 to Jesus, in heaven, after he accomplishes atonement for sins but before he sits down, let's go back and see how the whole scene unfolds. Jesus appears before God the Father and all the angels, having atoned for sin. The first thing the Father says is directed toward Jesus: "*You* are my Son!" Notice how the pronouns change in the second half of Hebrews 1:5. God says the same thing, but this time he speaks not to the Son but to the

---

[6]Among many others, see Ardel B. Caneday, "The Eschatological World Already Subjected to the Son: The Οἰκουμένη of Hebrews 1.6 and the Son's Enthronement," in *A Cloud of Witnesses: The Theology of Hebrews in Its Ancient Contexts*, ed. Richard Bauckham et al., Library of New Testament Studies 387 (London: T&T Clark, 2008), 28-39.

[7]If your sense of Jesus being both divine and human is getting fuzzy, feel free to stop here for a moment and go to the "Getting Deeper: Christology" section at the end of the book. Short version: I am *not* saying that Jesus stopped being God when he became human (or that he stopped being human and went back to being God at the ascension). Nothing could be further from the truth.

angels: "*He* is my Son!" And continuing to address the inhabitants of heaven, he says, "Worship *him!*" Then, in Hebrews 1:7-12, God will explain to the Son why this should be so. "Angels," he says, "are my servants who will be whatever I want them to be; the only thing I want you to be is a king whose rule is permanent and unchanging" (Heb 1:7-9). "You [the Son] existed before them, you created them, and you will outlast them; you are the eternal Creator, and they are part of the finite creation" (Heb 1:10-12). "And because this is all true," God concludes, "take a seat" (Heb 1:13). The final words of Hebrews 1 are the author's, not God's, but they form a fitting climax to the scene. The Son will take his seat and rest, but the gathered assembly, those who are "ministering spirits sent to serve" (Heb 1:14), will now get back to work.

Once more, then, the sequence of Hebrews 1:5-14. Having accomplished atonement, Jesus is brought before the heavenly assembly and declared by God to be his Son. The angels are then commanded to worship him because he is their Creator and Lord, while they are created servants. Finally, the Son is invited to sit and does so, while the angels are dismissed to continue their ministries. The two main events from Hebrews 1:1-4 bracket all that God says in Hebrews 1:5-14: atonement → God speaks [Son—"worship him"—"you're the eternal king; they're created servants"—"sit"] → enthronement.

The Old Testament in Hebrews 1

Before moving on, we should take note of what Hebrews is doing with the Old Testament here. First, every single word that God the Father spoke to Jesus at his ascension is taken directly from the Old Testament. If Hebrews is about Jesus calling us to leave behind the old and move on with the new, wouldn't you expect the conversation that got us headed in that direction to draw from a different source? And maybe even more surprising is that not only is every word spoken by the Father *to Jesus* in Hebrews taken from the Old Testament, but so is every word spoken *by Jesus* in Hebrews (for example, Heb 2:12-13; 10:5-8).

Second, most of the texts cited here have—in their original contexts—something to do with the enthronement of the Davidic king on Mount

Zion, in Jerusalem (Ps 2:7; 45:7; 110:4; 2 Sam 7:14).[8] The New Testament regularly calls Jesus the son of David and the king of Israel, so it isn't strange that Hebrews would describe his enthronement using promises that God made to David and liturgies that Israel recited when David's sons took their thrones. But this king hasn't been established in Jerusalem but in heaven. Capital cities on mountains were often connected to heaven in ancient thought, and kings were regularly depicted as representatives of God/gods, but the effect of that connection was that the earthly king was legitimated *by* heaven, not that the king actually reigned *in* heaven and over heaven's inhabitants. So, Hebrews is citing these Old Testament texts in a way that resonates deeply with their original use and yet relocates them from Jerusalem to heaven.

Third, if you've spent much time reading other parts of the New Testament, the last quote in Hebrews 1 probably sounded familiar. Psalm 110:1—"The Lord [God] said to my lord [David's Son]: 'Sit at my right hand until I make your enemies a footstool for your feet.'" This verse is quoted or referenced more times, across more books of the New Testament, than any other part of the Old Testament (see, e.g., Mt 22:44; 26:64; Mk 12:36; Acts 2:34; 5:31; 7:55; Rom 8:34; Eph 1:20; Col 3:1; 1 Pet 3:22). It is hinted at in Hebrews 1:3 ("he sat down at the right hand of the Majesty in heaven") and quoted in Hebrews 1:13, and it will continue to be used throughout Hebrews to refer to the pivotal moment when Jesus took his seat at God's right hand. The other pivotal Old Testament text, which we'll deal with in part two, is Psalm 110:4: "The Lord [God] has sworn and will not change his mind: 'You are a priest forever like Melchizedek!'" Notice how the two verses of Psalm 110 correspond to the two critical moments of the story: atonement (Ps 110:4) and enthronement (Ps 110:1). Little wonder that some scholars have suggested that Hebrews is a sermon on Psalm 110.[9] That's probably an

---

[8]Randall C. Gleason, "Angels and the Eschatology of Heb 1–2," *New Testament Studies* 49 (2003): 92; Susan Docherty, *The Use of the Old Testament in Hebrews: A Case Study in Early Jewish Bible Interpretation*, Wissenschaftliche Untersuchungen zum Neuen Testament 2/260 (Tübingen: Mohr Siebeck, 2009), 150.

[9]The most recent participant in this conversation is Jared Compton, *Psalm 110 and the Logic of Hebrews*, Library of New Testament Studies 537 (London: T&T Clark, 2015).

oversimplification, but it shows you just how important this psalm is going to be for the whole argument of Hebrews.

If you're wondering what the point of all this is, don't give up yet. Hebrews 1 is primarily about the fact that God spoke *to* and *through* his Son, who happens to be awesome. The Son made everything, he sustains everything, and he inherits everything. Angels worship him as he sits enthroned in heaven. Not bad. But the last verse of Hebrews 1 hints that there's a bit more to the story: "Are not all angels ministering spirits, sent out to serve those who will inherit salvation?" The Son inherits everything, but also there are other heirs who will inherit salvation. Angels worship the Son, but they also serve his fellow heirs—those people whom he will call "brothers and sisters" (Heb 2:12). So Hebrews 1 is about Jesus, but apparently it's also about us. *We* will inherit. *We* will reign. *We* will stand in the presence of God and be called "sons and daughters." How does that work, and when does that happen? On to Hebrews 2.

Study Questions

1. Is there a story that you love to get lost in? What is it about *that* world that you find so appealing or interesting?

2. Do you read the Old Testament with the assumption that it doesn't matter anymore or that God isn't like that anymore?

3. Have you ever tried to picture the event of Jesus' arrival in heaven before? Did it look in your head anything like it looks in Hebrews 1?

2

JESUS AND HIS SIBLINGS

THE TECHNICAL TERM IS narcissistic personality disorder. Experts debate the location of the line between the disorder and the general tendency of every one of us to put ourselves at the center of the universe. In that general sense, at least, we're *all* narcissists.

Theologians have long spoken of humanity *incurvatus in se*—"curved in on oneself." It means the only thing in the world that I can see is *me*. And when all I can see is myself, my only orientation toward everyone else is that they should be just as interested in me as I am, which means the only contribution *you* make is what you offer *me*.

We all do this. We all have a propensity to treat everyone around as means to our ends. We all stand ready to suck the life out of others, to become clinging, manipulating, boundary-less leeches desperately hoping to receive from our friends or family what they were never meant to give. We are fetuses in the fallopian tube, grasping at the available nutrients and growing, growing, until the tube ruptures and death pours forth. You've been on the receiving end of such destructive behavior. You've also been the perpetrator of it.

Why do we do this? Relationships with others are precisely where God invites us to find direction and meaning and life. And life giving isn't meant to be a zero-sum game. It's meant to be one person receiving the free gift of life from another, *and vice versa*. Mutually beneficial exchange. But we feel the walls closing in and we react, we grasp, we strike, we rage against the claustrophobia of the soul that threatens to squeeze the life out of us completely. In desperation, we steal what could have been freely given.

Fear. Economists call it a scarcity mindset. It could be financial scarcity, but it also could be relational scarcity—scarcity of community, scarcity of the good that God has for us through mutually beneficial relationships with other people. And ultimately, fixation on that scarcity drives us to fear. Fear of loneliness. Fear of isolation. Fear of being cut off from the life-giving interaction for which God designed us. And in fear we are like the person in deep water who not only cannot save themselves but also manages to drown their rescuer.

Hebrews 2 will show us a better way. Part of that way is the straight-forward acknowledgment of our location: we do indeed live in a lifeless world. Part of that way is recognition that Jesus has entered into our ectopicness, he has taken on our isolation, our loneliness, our death. And part of it is that he has overcome that death and in doing so offered us life once more. Life as his siblings, life in community, life in service and stewardship, life as the sons and daughters of God.

This Isn't Just About Jesus (Hebrews 2:1-4)

The first few verses of Hebrews 2 are a quick aside, of sorts—"By the way, what I'm telling you is *really* important, so pay attention!" But if we read them as originally written, without chapter numbers or section headings or any break at all between Hebrews 1:14 and Hebrews 2:1, we'll see some connections that will guide us as we read the rest of Hebrews 2. The key word to notice is *salvation*, which appears in Hebrews 1:14 and Hebrews 2:3. Especially for those who are familiar with the Bible and comfortable with Christian language, it is easy to assume that we know what salvation is. But it's crucial to let the writer of Hebrews mean what *he* means by that word instead of assuming that it means what we've always understood it to mean. This is what the rest of Hebrews 2 is about, but here are two preliminary observations to get us started.

First, salvation is something that some people will "inherit" (Heb 1:14). That should send us back to the beginning of the book, where Jesus is the one who will inherit everything (Heb 1:2), just as he has already inherited the name Son (Heb 1:4). Jesus, apparently, is not the only person who stands to gain from all this. Hebrews 1 is not simply a story about one special person, the Son, who did some things and then lived happily ever after. It's also about how other people benefit from what the Son did—how they inherit something just like he inherited something.

Second, salvation is not something we want to ignore (Heb 2:3). We'll spend more time on this point in part three, when we look at Hebrews in relation to Israel's experience with God at Mount Sinai and in the wilderness outside the Promised Land. But as we come into the rest of Hebrews 2, we should keep this in mind: whatever constitutes salvation in this context—that is what is at stake for the audience of Hebrews as they decide whether to continue following Jesus.

Jesus Is Still Human (Hebrews 2:5-18)

Once again, let your eyes skip over the headings in your Bible (and in this book!) and see the flow from Hebrews 2:4 to Hebrews 2:5-6 ("For it was not to angels that God subjected the world to come, about which we are speaking"). Notice he describes this topic as the one "about which we are speaking"—meaning, we aren't starting a new discussion here. We're still having the same conversation as before, still talking about the Son, his name, his inheritance, his exaltation over the angels, all that. How exactly is what comes next going to relate to what's come before? Check out that little word *for* at the beginning of Hebrews 2:5. The whole argument of Hebrews 2:1-4 is being explained: this (Heb 2:1-4) is true *because* it was not to angels that God subjected the world to come. In other words, we really should not neglect our salvation, that is, our inheritance, *because* there is a world in the future that God has not given to angels. In fact, as we'll find out in the next few verses, God has not subjected this future world to angels because he has subjected it to *us*. That future world, in other words, is the promised inheritance "about which we are speaking." And there's that troublesome word translated "world" again (remember Heb 1:6?). But this time it's not simply a world but a "world to come"—an inhabited space that does not yet exist, or is not yet established, or something like that.

At the beginning of Hebrews 2:6 we find the next logical step in the argument: "Rather, it has been testified somewhere. . . ." What comes next, a long quote from Psalm 8, is going to substantiate the previous claim, in Hebrews 2:5, that the realm to come is going to be ruled by someone other than angels.

> What is mankind that you are mindful of them,
> a son of man that you care for him?
> You made them a little lower than the angels;
> you crowned them with glory and honor and put everything
> under their feet. (Heb 2:6-8, citing Ps 8:4-6)

Right after the quote we get Hebrews' initial commentary on the psalm: "By putting everything under them, God left nothing that is not subject to them. Right now, though, we don't see everything subject to them" (Heb 2:8). The psalm says God gave humanity glory and honor and dominion over everything (except the angels), but there's a problem: it doesn't take a genius to look around the world and recognize that humanity is not fulfilling that role particularly well. So, to back up for a moment and make sure we know where we are in the argument, we know that God has not subjected the future world to angels because the psalm says God subjected the present creation (except the angels) to humanity, even though the present creation isn't actually subject to humanity. Something's missing in the logic, isn't it? The missing piece appears in Hebrews 2:9, which says that even though we *don't* see humanity exercising dominion over God's creation as he originally intended, we *do* see Jesus exercising a particular kind of dominion: "We do see Jesus, who was made a little lower than the angels, now crowned with glory and honor." So far, then: Psalm 8 is proof that angels *won't* rule over the future world, for two reasons: (1) because it says humans were originally set up to rule over the earth and (2) because Jesus is ruling over heaven and its angelic inhabitants (see Heb 1).

How Things Were, Are, and Will Be

Maybe the simplest way forward is to chart how the governance of God's creation works at different points in time. Here's how things started off, according to Psalm 8.

Table 2.1.

TIME: CREATION
GOD
ANGELS
HUMANITY
EVERYTHING ELSE

Pretty simple: God created everything, and humanity is rather fortunate to be above every other created thing, except the angels. But, of course, this structure didn't last. Hebrews doesn't go into the details of what exactly went wrong, but we might suggest two points of dysfunction: first, that in Hebrews 2:8 "everything else" is not currently subjected to humanity, and second, a bit more tentatively, that the "little" gap between angels and humanity has been stretched out of proportion. Later in Hebrews 2, we will learn that the devil (an angelic being) "holds the power of death" and enslaves humanity to the fear of death (Heb 2:14-15). Surely anyone who describes slavery as one person being a *little* lower than another has no idea what it means to be enslaved. So, the problematic part of the equation is at least about humanity in relation to all that should be below it, and possibly about humanity in relation to the angels above it as well.

Table 2.2.

TIME: FALLEN REALITY
GOD
ANGELS
HUMANITY VS. EVERYTHING ELSE

The first step in repairing the broken hierarchy is the coming of Jesus. When he came, he called other humans "brothers and sisters" (Heb 2:12), he "shared in their humanity" (Heb 2:14), and he "was made like them, fully human in every way" (Heb 2:17). And in doing all this, he "was made a little lower than the angels" (Heb 2:9). So now the chart looks like this:

Table 2.3.

TIME: INCARNATION
GOD
ANGELS
HUMANITY/JESUS
EVERYTHING ELSE

There's a lot we could say about how God remains on top of the hierarchy and yet Jesus remains God while becoming human and lowering himself. For now, we just need to be really clear: the first step toward fixing humanity's place in the created order is for God himself, in Jesus, to join humanity in that created order.

Then, of course, Jesus gets crowned with glory and honor above the angels. We can go back to Hebrews 1 to see how this happened in real time.

Table 2.4.

TIME: ASCENSION/ENTHRONEMENT
GOD/JESUS
ANGELS
HUMANITY
EVERYTHING ELSE

It's a bit anticlimactic, to be honest. What's been accomplished? Jesus comes down, Jesus goes back up, and there's no reason to think that anything changed for humanity. Nice for Jesus, but not much benefit to us.

Table 2.5.

TIME: FALLEN REALITY	TIME: ASCENSION/ENTHRONEMENT
GOD	GOD/JESUS
ANGELS	ANGELS
HUMANITY	HUMANITY
EVERYTHING ELSE	EVERYTHING ELSE

It looks like nothing has really changed. But notice that the phrase "glory and honor" describes both what humanity received when God put them over his creation (Heb 2:7) and what Jesus received when he was exalted in heaven (Heb 2:9). So "glory and honor" used to mean "rule earth but not the angels," but now it means "rule heaven and the angels."

Table 2.6.

TIME: CREATION	TIME: ASCENSION/ENTHRONEMENT
ANGELS	
HUMANITY ("GLORY AND HONOR")	JESUS ("GLORY AND HONOR")
EVERYTHING ELSE	ANGELS

Now go back to the original argument: angels won't rule over the world to come, because Psalm 8 says humans were supposed to rule over the earth (not heaven, since angels are there and they outrank us) and because Hebrews 1 says Jesus is ruling over heaven and its angelic inhabitants. Wouldn't it have been simpler to say, "Angels won't rule over the future world because Jesus will," and be done with it? Why say anything at all about the created order, humans just below angels, and so on? Psalm 8 is only relevant—and here's something so obvious you might miss it—*if*

Jesus, in his current state of dominion over heaven and its angelic inhabitants, is still human.[1] A human being walked into heaven and was presented to the angels as God's Son, as King of heaven, as heir of everything that exists, and he sits there now waiting for his Father to finish the job.

Think on that for a moment. First of all, if Jesus *isn't* still human, Psalm 8 just doesn't add anything to the argument. He came, he saw, he conquered, he went back to business as usual. Whatever this future world is, it's under Jesus' control because he's sitting enthroned at God's right hand and the angels are worshiping him because he's going to inherit *everything.* Sounds like a pretty decent gig. There just wasn't any reason to mention the created order in the first place.

Second, if Jesus isn't still human, none of this has done us any good. And since the whole point of this chapter is to unpack the salvation that's apparently so important, there must be some benefit to humanity at the end of all this.

Third, if Jesus *is* still human, there's a flesh-and-blood human being reigning over the "inhabited space" of heaven right now. *Over* the angels. Which means a human person has not only regained his position over God's creation, a little lower than the angels, but actually *improved* on it. Now, in heaven, a human being has been crowned with glory and honor *above* the angels, not below them.

Getting Ready to Rule

Here's the story so far: Jesus, who created everything and sustains everything, became human. He became part of the created order and therefore, by virtue of being human, became a little lower than the angels he created. But after he accomplished atonement, *while still remaining human* he was crowned with glory and honor by his Father and set above the angels. Notice the chronology of all this from the twin fulcrums of atonement and enthronement. First he becomes human. Then he *accomplishes atonement.* Then he is exalted above the angels. Then he

---

[1] If this surprises you, keep reading—and when you have a moment, check out "Going Deeper: Christology" at the end of the book.

sits. And the critical piece of the story at this point is that the first condition, becoming human, never goes away. He never stops being human, even when he is seated at his Father's right hand. So even though Psalm 8 isn't being fulfilled by anyone else, it is being fulfilled—and then some—by Jesus: "We do see Jesus, made a little lower than the angels, now crowned with glory and honor" (Heb 2:9).

Still, all well and good for Jesus, you might be thinking—what about us? That someone like me (i.e., human) is exalted above the angels might make me feel better, but it doesn't actually change my situation. If someone from my high school swim team competes in the Olympics, I've got some bragging rights—but I don't automatically become a better swimmer. But wait—look at the next verse. "In bringing many sons and daughters to glory, it was fitting that God, for whom and through whom everything exists, should make the pioneer of their salvation perfect through what he suffered" (Heb 2:10). Two things to see here. First, the Son isn't the only one who is going to get glory, just like, as we saw in Hebrews 1, he isn't the only one who is going to inherit something. There are other heirs—other "sons and daughters." Second, Jesus is described as a pioneer. A pioneer is different from, say, an explorer. An explorer goes off to new places and then might or might not come back to tell other people about what they've seen. A pioneer comes back and says, "Okay, now that I know where I'm going, who's coming with me?" A pioneer might be the first person to get from A to B, but they're not the last.

The question then becomes: What's A, and where's B? Where exactly is it that Jesus is going to lead others from, and where is he taking them to? This verse calls the destination salvation, and we already know from the beginning of Hebrews 2 that salvation is about the inheritance. And since the whole point of this part of Hebrews is that angels aren't going to rule the future world but that God originally set up humanity over his creation, and that right now there is a human person who has inherited the throne of heaven, and that reign is described as his glory, and his vocation—as a pioneer—is to lead others into the glory of their inheritance. . . . Do you see where this is going? Those of us who follow Jesus are going to share his glory just like he shared in our humiliation. We're going to govern the future world and its inhabitants, including angels.[2]

Ah, but what exactly *is* this future world? It isn't earth, or at least earth alone, because that's already here. But neither is it heaven, or at least heaven alone, for the same reason. The author of Hebrews doesn't tell us exactly what he has in mind here, but we can put a few lines of evidence together.

First, not even Jesus has received his full inheritance. He has been named as heir (Heb 1:2), but that's not the same as actually getting the inheritance. He's been invited to sit, but only until all his enemies have been subjected to him (Heb 1:13)—in other words, not all of them have been subjected yet.

Second, then, it cannot be the case that we join Jesus in glory in heaven, while earth—as we are so often led to believe—simply disappears from the scene. Were that true, there would be nothing left for Jesus to inherit beyond what he already has.[3]

Third, Hebrews has identified three distinct spheres: the material universe, heaven, and the world to come. If neither of the first two is going away completely, they must both in the end be within the borders of Jesus' kingdom—or Hebrews couldn't call him the heir of *everything*. And unless God is going to create a new third space in the future, alongside earth and heaven the only logical possibility we have left is that the world to come is neither heaven nor earth, nor something distinct from both, but rather the combination of the two. Hebrews doesn't spell this out for us, but it is exactly what we see happening at the end of Revelation: not us going up to heaven and leaving earth behind but

---

[2]Don't miss that Heb 1:14 says angels *already* serve those who *are about to* inherit salvation. Like so many other places in the New Testament, Hebrews preserves a tension between our already being saved and secure in Christ and our still anticipating the final touches on that salvation.

[3]Jon C. Laansma, *"I Will Give You Rest": The "Rest" Motif in the New Testament with Special Reference to Mt 11 and Heb 3–4*, Wissenschaftliche Untersuchungen zum Neuen Testament 2/98 (Tübingen: Mohr Siebeck, 1997), 140.

rather heaven and earth being made new and coming together (Rev 21:1-2). The closest Hebrews will get to this image is when it says that both heaven and earth will be shaken and transformed so that we can receive our inheritance: an unshakable kingdom (Heb 12:26-28). That kingdom is the future world that God has subjected to us rather than to the angels; it is the one realm, including both the renewed heaven and the renewed earth, that constitutes the whole inheritance of Jesus into which he will someday come.

We can't yet see all this, of course, but we have a faithful pioneer who guarantees it will happen. First, he names us his siblings even as he takes up his work of atonement: "I [Jesus] will tell of your [God's] name to my *brothers and sisters* [those others who will be brought to glory]; in the midst of the assembly I will sing your praises" (Heb 2:12). No son who plans on keeping the inheritance all to himself would ever publicly call other people his brothers and sisters.

Second, he made sure that he came all the way down to our level—it's no good promising to lead people on a trail if they can't find the trailhead in the first place: "Since the children have flesh and blood, he too shared in their humanity. . . . He had to be made like them, fully human in every way" (Heb 2:14, 17).

Third, he endured the very experience that makes us slaves rather than masters: he died so that he could "break the power of the one who holds the power of death—that is, the devil—and free those who all their lives were held in slavery by the fear of death" (Heb 2:14-15). There might be lots of ways to lead someone down a path that they wouldn't or couldn't take on their own, but none of them involve the leader staying behind and making their followers go ahead alone. In fact, if Jesus hadn't taken that specific path, not only would *we* not have arrived, but *he* wouldn't have either: he is "now crowned with glory and honor *because* he suffered death" (Heb 2:9).

Jesus came down to our level and recognized us as his co-heirs even before he took his throne, knowing even then that the path to that throne went right through the cross. And our section wraps up by saying that he did all this "so that he might become a merciful and faithful high priest in service to God, and that he might make atonement for the sins of the people. Because he himself suffered when he was tempted, he is able to help those who are being tempted" (Heb 2:17). See how we keep coming back to our two key moments? Atonement and enthronement, time and time again. So, now that we've come to the end of this chapter, here's the whole story of Jesus, according to Hebrews 1–2:

Create everything → become human → recognize others as future heirs → be tempted and suffer → become a high priest → accomplish atonement → be presented to angels as Son and heir and be invited to sit → sit → inherit everything.

The point of this story, as far as we are concerned, is that Jesus didn't become human for a little while and then stop being human later. He's still one of us. That means he gets what we're going through and can't wait to help, but it also means he's gone where we're trying to go and has made it possible for us to go there as well.

Study Questions

1. Is it odd for you to think of Jesus still being human, even now that he's in heaven? Why might it be so important that he is still human?

2. How might it reshape our vision of eternity to include redeemed humans, ruling over all of God's creation, in that vision?

3

FEELING OUT OF PLACE?

HEBREWS 1–2 TELLS A LOT OF GOOD NEWS. Jesus is alive, Jesus is enthroned, Jesus has died and was raised and accomplished atonement, Jesus has restabilized the created order and even upgraded our position in it, Jesus has identified us as his siblings who will inherit salvation and reign over the new creation with him. Talk about a happy ending.

Hebrews is optimistic about the future. It's also realistic about the present. "Right now we do not see all things subject to him" (Heb 2:8). "In this world you will have trouble," as Jesus says in John 16:33. Trouble because we aren't governing over creation properly. Trouble because Jesus' enemies have not yet been subjected to him. Trouble because death still lurks. Death in God's good world, a world that was designed to be a place of life for us and for the rest of his creation. "Right now we do not see. . . ." It might as well say, "Right now we cannot *live.*" Hebrews is confident that one day we will live precisely as God intended us to live, but it is honest about the fact that we do not yet live in that way. But what are we supposed to do between now and then? How do we live in a world that still reeks of death?

God spoke. That's the main thing. Sometimes the Father speaks to the Son (like in Heb 1:8-9). Sometimes the Son speaks to the Father, like in Hebrews 2:12. Jesus says, "I will declare your name to my brothers and sisters; in the assembly I will sing your praises." Back in Hebrews 1, it turned out to be pretty important *when* the Father spoke those words to the Son. That's true here as well. Jesus is quoting Psalm 22:22, so let's go back to the psalm itself to see how that story unfolds.

Psalm 22 is a lament, which means the writer is going through a bad time and asking God to do something about it. There are a lot of laments in the Psalms, and most of them, like Psalm 22, end on some sort of happy note—"Please help me. . . . Thank you for helping me!" Psalm 22 is one of the more dramatic happy-ending laments, because it doesn't just have a postscript indicating that God has come through; it has ten whole verses of praise tacked on the end. Our verse, the one Jesus quotes according to Hebrews 2:12, is the first verse of those ten—it's the beginning of the praise.

Our question is, When would Jesus have said these words? Well, if we read the first part of Psalm 22, we'll see some familiar lines. "My God, my God, why have you forsaken me?!" (Ps 22:1). "All who see me mock me; they hurl insults, shaking their heads. 'He trusts in the LORD,' they say, 'let the LORD rescue him. Let him deliver him, since he delights in him'" (Ps 22:7-8). "They divide my clothes among them and cast lots for my garment" (Ps 22:18). Sounds a lot like Jesus dying on the cross (see Mt 27:39, 43, 46). So Jesus and the Gospel writers are telling us that the human experience recounted by David in Psalm 22 is the part of God's word to us and our words to God that is most fitting to be spoken as Jesus' experience of death. Jesus is surrounded by enemies, he has cried out to God but God has not answered, and he is about to die.

But then comes our verse, Psalm 22:22, and Jesus is suddenly singing his Father's praises. Well, sort of. He's not singing God's praises in Psalm 22:22—he's saying that he *will* sing God's praises at the proper time and in the proper place. In Psalm 22:1-21, there's a lot of emphasis on *where* the psalmist is: far from God (Ps 22:1-2, 19), far from supporters (Ps 22:11), surrounded by enemies (Ps 22:6-7, 12-13, 16-18, 20-21). Wherever he is, he's definitely *not* in the company of friends. But in Psalm 22:22, he's talking about being "in the assembly" and with "my people." What's going on? Most likely, Psalm 22:22 is the psalmist saying, "Right now I'm not in a good spot, but I'm confident that one day I will be; right now

God isn't coming through for me, but I'm confident that one day he will; right now I experience nothing but pain and death, but I'm confident that one day I will experience life in all its fullness—and on that day I'm going to invite everyone around me to join in praising God for his deliverance!" And then the specific things that he will say about God at that time are given in Psalm 22:23-31.[1]

This is quite extraordinary—while still suffering, the psalmist says, "Not only am I confident that one day I will be delivered, not only am I confident that when that happens I'll have the chance to be surrounded by friends instead of enemies and invite them to praise God with me, but I am so confident of all this that I'll tell you right now the very things I plan to say about God when I have the chance." And while Hebrews doesn't go into those specific things, I can't help but notice one of them, in Psalm 22:29: "All the rich of the earth will feast and worship; all who go down to the dust will kneel before him—those who cannot keep themselves alive." That's us, in that last part. We are those who cannot keep themselves alive. Death is coming for us. It's inevitable. It came for David, who wrote these words. It came for Jesus, who spoke them on the cross. It comes for us.

But here is the beautiful thing, the glorious thing happening in Hebrews 2:12, when Jesus names *us* as those who will stand in the assembly and respond to his invitation to praise the Father. "It is not the dead who praise the LORD," says Psalm 115:17. That's right. But we will praise him, because we will live. We will *live*. Jesus on the cross says, "Father, I will yet praise you, and I will do so in the company of many others whom I call brothers and sisters [Heb 2:11], because *I* will live, and therefore so will they."

- This book is about *living ectopically*—living in an environment that ought to kill us, that can't sustain us. Hebrews 2 suggests that the reason living in a lifeless world is possible in the first place is that Jesus "by the

---

[1]English Bibles vary on how they translate the end of Ps 22:21, and it makes a fair bit of difference to the point being made in those verses. If you're interested in the details, see Michael H. Kibbe, "'You Have Answered Me?': Situational Shift (or Not) in Psalm 22," *Bulletin for Biblical Research* 34 (2024): 43-53.

grace of God tasted death for everyone" (Heb 2:9), and "by his death he broke the power of him who holds the power of death" (Heb 2:14). It starts with the recognition that life-from-without has conquered the death that reigns within.

Don't skip past this point. Don't say, "Oh, yeah, of course, Jesus rose from the dead, isn't that nice, back to my meaningless existence." Everywhere in the Bible, God's power is most overwhelmingly on display when he takes Death to its own woodshed.[2] Abraham's faith is built on "the God who gives life to the dead and calls into being things that were not" (Rom 4:17). Paul himself, under the burden of a psychological and legal death sentence, found hope only in "the God who raises the dead" (2 Cor 1:9). We'll get to Hebrews 11 later, but here's a little foreshadowing: the whole chapter is about living by faith in a God who speaks life where there is death. So don't move on too quickly from this point. If God can conquer death, if God can pour out life where all other springs have dried up, of whom should we be afraid?

Afraid. That's really the point, isn't it? It's not just that we're going to die someday. It's not just *death* that's the problem. It's the *fear* of death. This is why Hebrews 2:15 concludes the point about Jesus freeing us from *death* by saying that he "frees those who all their lives were held in slavery by their *fear* of death."

The American Psychological Association defines *fear* as "a basic, intense emotion aroused by the detection of imminent threat, involving an immediate alarm reaction that mobilizes the organism by triggering a set of physiological changes."[3] Fear is your brain telling your body that something unpleasant is coming your way. But this is tricky, because when God says, "Don't fear," he doesn't mean, "Tell your brain to quit telling your body that something unpleasant is coming your way." He

---

[2] The personification of Sin and Death in Romans is increasingly recognized in Pauline scholarship; for a recent and accessible account see Beverly Roberts Gaventa, *When in Romans: An Invitation to Linger with the Gospel According to Paul* (Grand Rapids, MI: Baker Academic, 2016), 23-46.

[3] "Fear," APA Dictionary of Psychology, updated April 19, 2018, https://dictionary.apa.org /fear.

doesn't mean, "Don't have physiological reactions to things that hurt." So what does he mean?

It helps to think about fear as having multiple phases.[4] Phase one: noticing that I'm having a physiological reaction in anticipation of pain. Nothing wrong with that—if I see my friend about to get run over by a truck, it would be good if I had a physiological reaction to that. If I'm about to speak in public, shortness of breath and increased heart rate are signals that what I'm about to do is important, not that I've made a mistake by being here in the first place.

Phase two: asking, *What prompted that response?* Why am I short of breath, and why is my heart rate going up? Is it because I've got a speech to give tomorrow? Is it because there's an angry person in my personal space? Or is it because I have past experiences that are coming back at me right now?

Phase three: asking, *Is my physiological reaction rational?* Am I afraid because there really is a mountain lion about to eat me, or am I afraid because I'm the sluggard who avoids going outside to work because there might be a lion in the streets (Prov 22:13)? It's not wrong to have a pit in my stomach while standing near a cliff, because it really would hurt to fall off that thing. But I have to stop and ask myself: What reasons are there to think that I *will* fall off that cliff, just because it's there?

Phase four: asking, *What would be a productive response?* If I'm afraid of failing a test tomorrow, studying might help. If I'm afraid of falling off that cliff, not doing cartwheels right next to it would be a good idea. If I'm afraid of public speaking, practice, practice, practice. All sorts of tips and tricks, and sometimes really simple things, help us overcome our fear—not in the sense that we'll necessarily quit experiencing the physiological part of fear but in the sense that we'll endure it and channel it into something productive. How many stories have you heard about people who become world class in some arena whose devotion to that craft began as a response to fear? Fear of failure can make us great. Fear

---

[4]Thanks to my clinical psychologist colleague Dr. Aryn Ziehnert for helping me think through this.

of pain can make us resilient. Fear of shame can make us secure. Or not, of course. But it's not the fear itself, the initial physiological response, that's the problem. It's what we do with it. And I think that's what Hebrews 2 is about. What do we do with our natural fearful reaction to death? What did Jesus do?

Once more: what Jesus did was *speak God's words*. Hebrews 2:12-13, quoting Psalm 22:22 and Isaiah 8:17-18. The first, Psalm 22:22, is his confession of faith that there is life beyond death, that he will praise God in the assembly at some point in the future, which necessarily means that the pain of death does not have the final word. We all know what it's like, during some difficult experience, to be unable to see that the world even exists beyond that experience. Jesus invites us to stare death in the face and say, "You are not the end of me. You might be painful, you might be scary, you might be awful. But I will endure beyond you."

The next two texts go together: Isaiah 8:17 and 8:18. "I will trust in him. . . . Here I am, along with the children God has given me." Isaiah is standing by as the people of Jerusalem lose their collective heads over an impending invasion, and God's promise to them in that moment is the arrival on the scene of three children: Shear-Jashub, whose name means something like "a remnant will return" (Is 7:3); "Immanuel," which means something like "God is with us" (Is 7:14); and Maher-Shalal-Hash-Baz, which means something like "quick to the plunder, swift to the spoil" (Is 8:1-4). Three sons, three names, three very particular promises of God for this terrifying moment in Israel's history. First son: no matter what happens, no matter how bad things get, there will always be a remnant. Second son: no matter what happens, no matter how bad things get, God will always be with you. Third son: no matter what happens, no matter how bad things get, God is going to deal with this situation so fast it will make your head spin. "Here I am," says Isaiah, "watching the story unfold, holding fast to the promises represented by the names of these children."

Imagine those three boys running around the chaos of war-torn Jerusalem, and every time someone calls out their names, the promises of

God are spoken anew. "Hey, Immanuel—time to come in for dinner!"
"Come on, Shear-Jashub, I need your help with the animals!" Their very
names are countertestimonies to our interpretation of the world around
us. Everything I see says, "God has forsaken you!" But I look at those
kids, and I think, *No, he hasn't.*

Jesus quotes those words in Hebrews 2:13—"Here I am, with the
children God has given me." But he isn't talking about Shear, Maher, and
Immanuel. He's talking about *us* (Heb 2:14-16). You and me. The ectopic
humans into whom he has infused his indestructible life, whose very
way of existing is a countertestimony to the fear that pervades the world
around us. And what way is that? The way of Jesus. The way that mourns,
as Jesus did, but does not mourn as though there is no hope. The way
that refuses to let fear of death become fear of the possibility of death,
which becomes fear of anything that hurts a lot, which becomes fear of
anything that hurts at all, which becomes fear of anything that might
hurt even the slightest bit. It's not wrong to fear (that is, have a physiological reaction to anticipation of) death. It is wrong to let that fear fester
and sink in and take such hold of us that we fall down the slope of
avoiding pain at all costs.

I don't want to oversimplify things here. Sometimes pain is just bad.
But most of the time pain is our bodies trying to tell us something. Pain
speaks different truths in different contexts. So does failure, so does
sickness, so do negative experiences such as rejection and anxiety and
poverty. Our avoidance of discomfort stems from a wrong belief that *life*,
life as it ought to be lived, means not experiencing things, whether
physical or emotional, that remind us of our mortality. We want to
pretend that we aren't ectopic in the first place.

But we *are* ectopic. We *are* out of place. This world *can't* keep us alive.
A misguided response to fear drives us to deny what we know to be
true—and what we know to be true is that death comes for us all. "Who
among you, by worrying, can add an hour to your lifespan?" (Mt 6:27).[5]

---

[5]Psychologists often distinguish between fear and anxiety/worry in two respects: fear is in
response to something immediate and specific (The bear standing in front of me is about
to eat me), while anxiety is distant and vague (What will happen to me if the stock market

Fear of death is already foolish if it drives us to avoid pain, because pain and death are inevitable. It is also foolish because death is a defeated enemy. Jesus stepped out of place with us—is there anything more ectopic than a loving Creator dying at the hands of his hateful creatures? The world to which he gave life in the first place, those image bearers whose life he gave and whose life he now shares, are trying to steal that life from him. But now he's come back into place, and that place is not only *his* place; it's ours as well. The only problem that remains is that we aren't there yet. "Right now we don't see everything subjected to humanity" (Heb 2:8).

What then? We are destined for death, and yet that is not the last word on the matter because Jesus has faced death, overcome death, and he now sits at God's right hand and invites us to join him as his brothers and sisters and fellow heirs of the new creation in which God will cause us to live. Death still comes, but I do not fear it. I can walk by faith in the God who does raise and will raise the dead. I can live a full and meaningful and risky and self-sacrificial life because "my life is hid with Christ on high, with Christ, my Savior and my God," as the great hymn puts it.[6] "I'm no longer a slave to fear, I am a child of God" (if you prefer songs of more recent vintage).[7]

I do not deny death, because I am in fact ectopic. But neither am I controlled by fear of death, because life comes to me from Jesus—Jesus who lived, who died, and who now lives again. And he lives not only for his own sake but for mine; he offers his life to me and calls me his sibling, beloved of his Father, and fellow human being destined for glory and honor when he returns and makes all things new.

I hope this prompts the question, Why? Put it in the terms of Psalm 8, where Hebrews 2 began: "Why, God, given how fantastically awesome and big and glorious you are, why would you care about humanity? Why would you put us in such a privileged position in your world?" (Ps 8:6-8).

---

collapses?). This is a helpful distinction, though I think the notion of fear in Heb 2 probably covers both experiences.
[6]"Before the Throne of God Above," lyrics by Charitie Lees Bancroft, music by Vikki Cook.
[7]Jonathan Helser and Melissa Helser, "No Longer Slaves," Bethel Music Publishing, 2014.

Why, indeed? And now we take that question up a notch: Why, after we threw your gift back in your face, would you not only renew your offer but even add to it? We have so much more to learn from Hebrews of God's love for us and our subsequent love for others, and the time will come, in a few chapters, for that to be the main topic of conversation. But while the word *love* is not found in Hebrews 2, let's not miss how prominent it is. Love is why the Son became lower than the angels. Love is why he endured our slavery to bring us freedom. Love is why the one who has been declared Son now declares us "sons and daughters." Love is why he helps us in our sufferings, encourages us in our temptations. Love is why he became like us so that we would become like him. Hebrews has much more to say about *how* this happened, and *when*, and *where*, and all the rest, but let's be mindful at the beginning of the *why*: because he loves us.

Study Questions

1. What do you fear?
2. Do you feel guilty for being afraid?
3. What helps you remember that God is with you even when you are legitimately afraid?

SECTION 2

JESUS' PROVISION OF LIFE

MY WIFE AND I HAD AN ARGUMENT the other day. It wasn't about anything particularly important. But I was mad, and she was mad, and, of course, this happened thirty seconds before I needed to put the kids in the car and take them to school. Classic. So we're standing in the kitchen, staring daggers at each other, and the kids are putting shoes and coats and backpacks on as they head out the door. And there's just no way we're resolving the issue right then and there. A perfunctory "Have a good day," and off we go in different directions.

I hate moments like that. I hate conflict anyway, but I really hate conflict that can't be resolved *now*. I hate having brokenness in my most important relationship hanging over my head all day long as I try to mentally focus on writing or teaching or grading or whatever task I have in front of me. All day long, I'm bouncing back and forth between frustration at Annie, frustration at myself, frustration at the situation, and frustration at the fact that I'm still thinking about that situation when I really need to be getting work done.

Annie and I have been together for nearly twenty years, so we've done this silly routine more than once. But two things have changed over time. The first is that a sudden change prompted a gradual shift. The sudden change was going from dating, courting, engaged, and so on, to being married. It was a sudden change because in that moment we made an unbreakable promise to each other, and so the fact is that neither of us is going to respond to an argument by simply deciding this relationship wasn't such a great idea after all. But it takes time for that fact to sink in, and so over the early months and years of marriage it became more and more apparent to both of us that we meant what we said in our vows.

The second change is related to the first, because not only did we grow in our awareness that we weren't going to give up on each other, but we also grew—and are continuing to grow—in our ability to function in the midst of the situation. I mean, it's one thing to stop being *afraid* that Annie will give up on me. It's another to manage the *frustration* I still experience when we have unresolved conflict. I don't experience that particular fear anymore. But I'm still very much in process when it comes to managing the frustration.

Part of the frustration management involves immediate action. Looking Annie in the eye just before I go out the door and saying, "I know we're mad; I know we need to revisit this. I love you, and I look forward to coming back together tonight to talk things through." Taking a moment to talk to the kids in the car, to say, "Hey, I know you saw that happen, and I want you to know that Mommy and I love each other, and we're going to sort things out when we have a chance. And, by the way, having conflict and then resolving conflict actually strengthens relation-ships—so Mommy and I are going to love each other even more when this is done than we did before it started."

Another part of the frustration management involves compartmen-talization. It takes mental discipline for me to put the conflict out of my mind and focus on the task at hand. I'm headed to the office, to the classroom, to the job site, to the meeting, whatever, and both God and Annie need me to focus on whatever is waiting for me in those locations rather than fixating all day on what happened at home this morning. I have to admit that I'm pretty lousy at this part of the equation. On this particular occasion, I managed to get us a coffee date midmorning, and we resolved things then. Awfully helpful at my current stage of maturity in this arena.

Here's the key, though: both the immediate action and the compart-mentalization only work if two things are true. First, it must be true that

Annie and I have an unbreakable commitment to each other. If our commitment is conditional, it isn't necessarily the case that this situation is going to be resolved, because one of us just might decide it isn't worth it. And second, it must be true that Annie and I will in fact reconvene that evening and refuse to let the sun go down on our wrath. If we don't eventually fix the problem, immediate action is pointless, and compartmentalization is just sweeping it under the rug.

The brokenness in my marriage is symptomatic of the brokenness of life in general. We are constantly in conflict, somewhere, with someone. The world is not as it should be, nor are the relationships that exist in it. There's *always* something wrong, something unresolved. And insofar as God designed us to give and receive life in and through those relationships, we constantly feel the lifelessness of being at the office when we'd rather be at home healing a rift in our marriage. Or, perhaps, we feel out of place in our own homes, in close physical proximity to those from whom we should be receiving life but aren't.

If the analogy from my marriage to life in general works, we need some immediate action and some compartmentalization. But that means, first, we need to know that two things are true: that something fundamental (like, marriage-vows fundamental) has already happened that guarantees final resolution, *and* that there is a plan in place for that final resolution to actually occur.

This part is mostly about the first truth: that something has happened in the past, something that changes everything, something that guarantees total resolution and reconciliation. Something akin to an unbreakable marriage vow. And just to be clear: that something won't imply that all is now well with the world, because it isn't. But it will imply that God will not stop pursuing resolution until he achieves it, that God will not under any circumstances give up on us, that the redemption of all things is in fact an attainable reality, and therefore we need not be consumed by fear or by frustration between now and then.

The something that God has done is what theologians call the atonement. *Atonement*, an odd word based on the idea of "at-one-ment," means the coming back together of what should never have been torn apart. God and us, for starters, but also you and me, each of us in our whole network of human relationships, and even the whole world, human and nonhuman alike. And the next part of this book is about how atonement works, how it happened, and why it matters.

4

PREPARING FOR
THE DEEP END

ATONEMENT CAN MEAN A LOT of different things. Scholars have suggested different buckets and categories and models to help us hold the whole thing together—maybe you've heard terms such as "penal substitution" or "*Christus Victor*," or words such as *redemption* and *justification* and *salvation* and *reconciliation* and *propitiation*, all of which are pointing—from different angles—in the general direction of "what God has done for us through Jesus."

It depends who you ask, but generally speaking the word *atonement* is either a catchall for the all of these terms and concepts put together, or it refers specifically to *sacrificial* (as opposed to *legal* or *relational* or *economic*) components of that larger category.[1] In Hebrews, it's usually the second option. Not that Hebrews doesn't care about legal (justification) or economic (redemption) components to God's work on our behalf, but when we see the word *atonement* in Hebrews, such as in Hebrews 2:17, where it says that Jesus "made atonement for the sins of the people," we're going to find ourselves talking about priests and sacrifices rather than courtrooms or battlefields or slave markets, such as

---

[1]Michael H. Kibbe, "Is It Finished? When Did It Start? Hebrews, Priesthood, and Atonement in Biblical, Systematic, and Historical Perspective," *Journal of Theological Studies* 65 (2014): 46.

we might find in Paul's letters. These different ideas aren't at all in conflict with one another; it's just that God has done a *lot* for us through Jesus, and not every part of the Bible is going to try to say all of it.[2]

Think back to the beginning of Hebrews, to the two main events in the whole story: *atonement* and *enthronement*. Jesus deals with the problem of sin, and Jesus sits at the right hand of God in heaven. Hebrews 1 told us about the enthronement scene itself, and Hebrews 2 told us that Jesus being human like us is why the enthronement scene is such a big deal, practically speaking. But that opening section of Hebrews says very little about the atonement part of the equation. What exactly did Jesus do, and why did it accomplish the at-one-ment of all that had been torn apart by sin?

Hebrews 1:3 says the Son accomplished purification for sins (sacrificial *atonement*) before he sat down—and then the sermon moves on to other things.[3] So all we know is that Jesus made atonement happen. Then, skipping ahead a bit, Hebrews 2:17 says one of the reasons the Son of God became human in the first place was so that he could be a "merciful and faithful high priest" and therefore "provide *atonement* for the sins of the people." Now we know that he accomplished atonement specifically in his role as high priest. It's crickets again for a couple more chapters, until Hebrews 4:14 suddenly says, "Since we have a great high priest (Jesus, the Son of God) who has entered heaven, let's hold on tightly to our faith!" This one doesn't mention *atonement*, but it names Jesus as high priest, and we've already been trained to put atonement and priesthood together by their earlier connection in Hebrews 2:17.

It's important to notice that both of these statements about Jesus as a high priest come at the end of major sections of Hebrews. Despite the fact that nothing in the preceding verses would have made you think, *Jesus is*

---

[2]For a broader overview of what the atonement is and how it works across the whole biblical witness, see "Going Deeper: Atonement" at the end of this book.

[3]Hebrews calls itself a "word of exhortation" (Heb 13:22), which many scholars have taken to mean "sermon." See especially Gareth L. Cockerill, *The Epistle to the Hebrews*, New International Commentary on the New Testament (Grand Rapids, MI: Eerdmans, 2012), 11-16.

my high priest!, the author of Hebrews wants us to begin considering how Jesus as a priest makes the rest of the argument work. Remember the story of Hebrews 2: God gave humanity a special place over creation, humanity forfeited that place, and Jesus has not only restored that place but actually taken his siblings up a level to rule over the new creation. And somehow that story climaxes with, "It's a good thing we have Jesus as our priest!" (Heb 2:17-18). The same is true of Hebrews 3–4: this long plea to persevere in faith rather than imitating the group of Israelites who forfeited the promises by rebelling at Kadesh Barnea (Num 13–14) concludes, again, with, "Thank goodness Jesus is our high priest in heaven!" (Heb 4:14-16). It's not yet obvious why Jesus' priesthood matters for these situations, but Hebrews wants us to start thinking in that direction.

At the end of Hebrews 4 and the beginning of Hebrews 5, the topic of Jesus as a priest-who-accomplishes-atonement comes up again, this time for good—almost. His presence in heaven encourages us to come to God when we need help resisting temptation (Heb 4:14-16). And on that note, the author of Hebrews says we'll start unpacking how he got to be a priest in the first place (Heb 5:1-10). High priests in general have some things in common: their job is to offer gifts and sacrifices to God (Heb 5:1), they identify with the weaknesses of those for whom they minister because they are similarly weak (Heb 5:2), they offer sacrifices for their own sins just like they do for the sins of others (Heb 5:3), and they get invited into the position by God, not at their own initiative (Heb 5:4).

It's this last point that matters most for how Jesus is a high priest like every other high priest: he did not exalt himself into the position of high priest. That was *God's* decision. Hebrews 5:5-6 quotes Psalm 2:7 again, just like it did back in Hebrews 1:5, so that we'll have the ascension in front of us, and then it says, "Remember who said, 'You are my Son!' to Jesus? The same one who said *that* also said, 'You are a priest forever!'" And remember how every word spoken by God the Father is drawn from the Old Testament? Same thing here: Hebrews 5:6, "You are a priest forever in the likeness of Melchizedek," is a citation of Psalm 110:4.

Psalm 110

Psalm 110:1 ("Sit at my right hand. . . .") is the most frequently cited Old Testament text in the New Testament. From very early on, beginning with Jesus himself, the person being addressed in Psalm 110 is identified as Jesus.[4] So, we'd better go back to Psalm 110 for a moment and see what's going on there.

If I could oversimplify things a bit, there are three kinds of psalms. There are praise psalms (God is great, God is good, everything is awesome), which are the ones we sing in church. There are lament psalms (I thought God was great, I thought God was good, but everything is *not* awesome), which are the ones we *should* sing in church but usually don't. Then there are weird psalms, which a lot of us wouldn't know how to sing in church even if we wanted to. And Psalm 110 is definitely in the third category. Actually, it falls into a category of psalms that exalt the Davidic king—which is definitely weird from our (democratic and monotheistic) vantage point.[5] You'll see in those psalms a bit of a triangular relationship: the exaltation of *God* is the exaltation of *Mount Zion* is the exaltation of *David and his descendants*.[6] Because two of God's fundamental promises to Israel are that he will dwell with them on his holy mountain and that he will rule through his chosen servant David, these three things go together.

Here's how this works in Psalm 110. First, most of the psalm is about God establishing the reign of the Davidic king: his enemies made a footstool (Ps 110:1), his scepter extended out from Zion (Ps 110:2), his troops ready for battle (Ps 110:3), kings and rulers and nations crushed in his wake (Ps 110:5-6). Second, there's a future orientation to nearly every line: his enemies are not yet a footstool for his feet (Ps 110:1), his scepter *will* be extended (Ps 110:2), the day of battle has not yet come

---

[4]For a little more data on how in the world the New Testament could read Ps 110:1 and think, "Oh, yeah, that's clearly about Jesus," see "Going Deeper: Hebrews and the Old Testament" at the end of this book.

[5]Take a look at Ps 2; 20; 72; 89 if you want to see how this works.

[6]On this point see especially Ben C. Ollenburger, *Zion, the City of the Great King: A Theological Symbol of the Jerusalem Cult*, Journal for the Study of the Old Testament Supplements 41 (Sheffield: JSOT Press, 1987).

(Ps 110:3), God *will* crush the kings and rulers and nations (Ps 110:5-6), and so forth. Third, the reign of the Davidic king involves the participation of others: there are troops involved in the battle (Ps 110:3), of course, but also Psalm 110:4—the Davidic king is a priest. And there's no point in having a priest if there isn't anyone else in the picture who needs a priest. Priests, as Hebrews 5:1 told us, exist to stand between God and his people—to "act on behalf of other people in relation to God."

Three things: the establishment of David's son as *king*, the *future* establishment of David's son as king, and the establishment of David's son as *priest*. At this point you should be thinking, *That sounds a lot like Hebrews!* Hebrews 1–2 hits all three of these things: Jesus established as king over heaven, Jesus not yet (but some day) established as king over earth, and the vague hint—just as Psalm 110:4 offers no more than a vague hint—that Jesus has also been established as priest. And this is the fascinating thing about Hebrews: Psalm 110:1 is everywhere in the New Testament, but only Hebrews mentions Psalm 110:4. And here in Hebrews 5:6 we find the very first mention of this verse: the one who said, "You are my Son!" (Ps 2:7) also said, "You are my priest!" (Ps 110:4).

Getting Ready to Be a Priest

Hebrews 5:7-10 describes the sequence of events that climaxed with Jesus being appointed as high priest. First, Hebrews 5:7 will probably remind you of Gethsemane, the cross, and the resurrection: he prayed "with fervent cries and tears" to the one who could save him from death, *and he was heard*. When did he pray like this? In the garden and on the cross, when he quoted Psalm 22. When was he heard and "saved from death"? At the resurrection. Why did God wait until then? Why didn't he rescue him from death in the way you and I might want to be rescued from death—that is, by preventing him from dying? Because, Hebrews 5:8 says, even though he was God's Son, he needed to "learn obedience through suffering," and that's how he "became perfect."

A couple of thoughts on this sequence. First, Jesus was God's Son already, so what happens later (chronologically) at the ascension, when the Father says, "You are my Son; *today* I have begotten you!" doesn't mean he wasn't God's Son until that point. It means he was *officially recognized* as God's Son at that moment.

Second, Jesus needed to learn things. Does that mean he gave up being the omniscient God? No. It means human experience was new to him. The Second Person of the Trinity, the Son, had never experienced the need to obey under the pressure of temptation and pain and human weakness.

Third, apparently he had to experience that pressure in order to "be made perfect" (Heb 5:9). But what in the world does *that* mean? Scholars typically go in one of two directions: (1) it's a word often used in Leviticus to denote the "appointability" of a priest—meaning, "he checks all the boxes for being qualified to serve as priest" (see Lev 16:32; 21:10); or (2) it denotes the ability of a person, whether Jesus or anyone else, to be in the presence of God (see Heb 7:19; 10:1).[7] Either way: it *doesn't* mean he was imperfect in the moral sense, as though he had sins up to that point and needed to be purified or perfected from them. Hebrews 4:15; 7:27 make that clear enough. But it *does* point to some element of his being qualified to serve as priest: if he isn't perfect, he can't be a priest. That's why the rest of Hebrews 5:9, along with Hebrews 5:10, says this: "Having been made perfect, he became the source for eternal salvation to all who obey him because he was now appointed by God as a priest like Melchizedek."

Here's the whole sequence of events: suffering/praying/obeying/ dying → rising → being perfected → being appointed as high priest → being the source of salvation (i.e., atonement). Because he suffered and died, and obeyed in the process, his prayer to be rescued from death was answered when God raised him from the dead. And because of all that, he was perfected and therefore became a high priest, and therefore provided salvation to others.

It's Time to Grow Up

We've ignored one big question, haven't we? Or should I say, the author of Hebrews has ignored one obvious question. That question appears as

---

[7]Benjamin J. Ribbens, *Levitical Sacrifice and Heavenly Cult in Hebrews*, Beihefte zur Zeitschrift für die neutestamentliche Wissenschaft 222 (Berlin: de Gruyter, 2016), 171-78.

soon as Psalm 110:4 does, as soon as it says Jesus is a priest "like Melchizedek." *Who in the world is Melchizedek, and why is he so important?* The author of Hebrews would love to get to that. He's the next item on the agenda. But, one more time, we get interrupted. And this time, it's not because the author wants to head off to some other topic and make us wait a while longer, like he did in Hebrews 1:3 and Hebrews 2:17 when the atonement and priesthood issues first came up. This time, it's because there's a problem with his audience.

> I've got a lot more to say about this, but it's hard to explain because you all have a hearing problem. You should be mature teachers and deeply engaged in the deep things of God, but you are practically infants in terms of your behavior. What I'm giving you here is steak, and you want a bottle of formula instead, because your spiritual jaw muscles haven't been strengthened by practicing what you've heard preached up to this point. (Heb 5:11-14)

We don't know exactly what was going on with the first readers of Hebrews. We don't know precisely what immature behavior they were manifesting. But we do know some things. We do know, from Hebrews 6:1-2, that the author of Hebrews considers repentance and faith, baptism and the laying on of hands (probably a reference to spiritual gifts and incorporation into the church), and the resurrection of the dead and final judgment, to be the milk, the ABCs of the Christian faith, that they have known for a long time but haven't been putting into practice. And we do know that anyone who fails to put into practice the basics of Christianity will be unable to grasp the deeper things of our faith. Again: It's not more *learning* that enables the deeper grasp. It's more *practice*. One more time, so we don't miss it: further education is no guarantee of further maturity.

I teach the Bible for a living. This is a big deal for me. My students and I spend an incredible amount of time studying God's Word. Our curriculum is set up, as all curricula must be, so that if you pass one class you can move on to the next. And it would be pretty tough, not to mention a little awkward for the accreditors, to grade students based on their obedience to what they've learned so far. We have to constantly remind ourselves that graduating with a degree in biblical studies, whether undergraduate or doctorate, is no guarantee of real growth in the faith. If we really want to go deep with God, we have to obey what we've learned so far. Only then can we move on.

There's something here worth noticing, beyond the specific things that apparently constitute the ABCs of Christian faith and life. It's something I think we can all relate to, and that is the feeling that we have not progressed, we have not matured in the ways or at the rate that we think we ought to have done. There's something deadening about this, actually, because God created us to work, to act, to achieve things and do things and make things happen, and he designed us to receive a sense of meaning and purpose and life from doing so. Dissatisfaction with our accomplishments can be a crippling, draining, life-stealing experience. And in the face of that experience, Hebrews 5 offers a critical word of encouragement if we would seek life where it can actually be found. That word is, *practice the basics.*

Why? Why would something as mundane as "practice the basics" be critical to life in a lifeless world? Because God did in fact create us to work and achieve and find satisfaction in doing so. So, the solution can't be apathy or laziness. But we are finite creatures receiving life from an infinite Creator, so that solution can't be the sort of god complex–inducing fame with which so many today are obsessed. Our invitation is to live *faithfully*, not necessarily *famously*. There's also a purely practical component to this: that infinite Creator, because he loves order, has arranged his creation so that all skills and crafts are a matter of basic principles endlessly extrapolated and applied. Music, sports, war, art, cooking, public speaking—every human endeavor works like this, and so it is entirely unsurprising that in every arena the greatest achievers are obsessed with the fundamentals. The deeper knowledge, the more complex movements, are simply outworkings of the basics. Our ability to wrestle with complexity is a function of our grasp of simplicity.

We, as sinners, are prone to thinking of ourselves more highly than we ought to think. That might mean thinking that we've accomplished more than we have or that we deserve more credit than is really our due. Or it might mean assuming that we are destined for greatness, that we can do anything if we set our minds to it, that we're going to change the world. And the fact, the glorious, liberating, life-giving fact, is that greatness by any worldly standard is neither necessary nor necessarily possible, as far as God is concerned. He has not asked this of us, and he may not have enabled this in us. What he has done is invited us into what some have called a "long obedience in the same direction."[8]

I am in my mid-forties. That means for me, as it probably does for many people my age, that I am beginning to appreciate both how long it takes to do anything worth doing and how unlikely it is that I'll live long enough to do most of the things I want to do. And so I have two choices: I can despair that life is so short and full of trouble, or I can lean into the basic, life-giving repetition of truths about God and the world he has created, trusting that faithfulness with little will lead to opportunities for faithfulness with much in his own good time.

Study Questions

1. Is it strange to think about Jesus as your priest? What comes to mind when you meditate on that?

2. Read Psalm 110. What strikes you about this unusual psalm?

3. What basic truths have you known as long as you can remember, but never really put into practice?

---

[8]I first heard this phrase in the title of Eugene Peterson's book (*A Long Obedience in the Same Direction: Discipleship in an Instant Society* [Downers Grove, IL: InterVarsity Press, 1980]), but Peterson borrowed it from Friedrich Nietzsche, *Beyond Good and Evil*, trans. Helen Zimmern (New York: The Modern Library, 1929), 98, 5.188.

5

JESUS OUR PRIEST

MELCHIZEDEK. PRIESTHOOD. SACRIFICE. Atonement. Ritual. We are about to swim in deep waters, which is why the author of Hebrews is upset that his audience hasn't sufficiently practiced the basic strokes. Hebrews 6 is primarily about the consequences of staying in the kiddie pool, and yet our author is confident that they're going to wake up and get to work, so that chapter ends with, "I'm going to go ahead and say what I was going to say about Melchizedek" (see Heb 6:20). In Hebrews 7, finally, we get to hear what the hype has been all about up to this point: Jesus is a priest like Melchizedek, and that's why the atonement happened in the first place.

Melchize-who?

The first time Melchizedek shows up in the Bible is in Genesis 14. He is "king of Salem and priest of God Most High" (Gen 14:18), he blesses Abraham (Gen 14:19-20), and Abraham gives him a tenth of all he has just collected in a major battle (Gen 14:20). The next time he is mentioned is Psalm 110:4, and the time after that is Hebrews 5:6. This guy is a mystery. One guest appearance in the life of Abraham, one extremely vague reference in the Psalms, and now, based on only those two moments, he's the star of Hebrews 7.

Let's talk about Melchizedek, king of Salem and priest of the God Most High, the one who met Abraham and blessed him when Abraham was returning from the slaughter of the kings, the one to whom Abraham gave a tenth of all his spoils [from the battle]. His name is first translated "king of righteousness," and, since he is king of Salem, it is also translated "king of peace." He has no father, no mother, and no genealogy, nor does he have any beginning of days or end of life; so, having been made like the Son of God, he remains a priest forever. (Heb 7:1-3)

A lot to take in here. The main thing for the moment is that last bit: no parentage, no family tree, and, because he was made like God's Son, an eternal priesthood. First, no father or mother or genealogy. Really? Who is this guy? Some think he's the pre-incarnate Son of God (what scholars call a Christophany)—but he's incarnate.[1] He's a flesh-and-blood person walking around. So he wouldn't be *pre*-incarnate; he'd be *incarnate*. So that doesn't work. Others think he's an angelic figure, a heavenly priest who shows up in the Old Testament as angels sometimes do. Other Jews in the New Testament period were asking questions about Melchizedek (it's hard to read Gen 14 and *not* have some questions!), and some speculated that he was the high priest of an angelic priesthood that served God in his heavenly temple.[2] Maybe. But it would be pretty awkward for the logic of Hebrews if Jesus' priesthood were an angelic one after all that emphasis in Hebrews 1–2 that Jesus is God and man, and precisely *not* an angel. So, the final and most likely option: the author of Hebrews is riffing on a common way of reading the Old Testament in his day called *non in tora, non in mundo*—if it's not in the Torah, it's not in the world.[3] In other words, if the Scriptures don't mention it, it might as well not exist. And when it comes to being a priest, your parentage is crucial.

---

[1]Amy L. B. Peeler, *Hebrews*, Commentaries for Christian Formation (Grand Rapids, MI: Eerdmans, 2024), 187.

[2]David M. Moffitt, *Atonement and the Logic of the Resurrection in the Epistle to the Hebrews*, Supplements to Novum Testamentum 141 (Leiden: Brill, 2011), 203-7.

[3]Luke T. Johnson, "The Scriptural World of Hebrews," *Interpretation* 57 (2003): 244.

According to the Old Testament, if you're not from the tribe of Levi, you're not a priest. Period. And yet here's a guy who—in terms of the narrative—isn't just not from the tribe of Levi; he's from no tribe at all. So he's an ancestry-less priest, which is both a stark exception to the biblical pattern and absolutely critical for what Hebrews is going to say about Jesus.

Hebrews 7:4-10 simply makes the point that since Melchizedek blesses Abraham in their encounter in Genesis 14, and Abraham gives a tenth (tithes) to Melchizedek, it's pretty clear who is superior to whom. Melchizedek > Abraham. And since Levi is descended from Abraham, Melchizedek > Levi. And since Melchizedek and Levi are the priestly prototypes in question, Melchizedekian priests > Levitical priests.

Now we come to the main issue. Hebrews has already identified Jesus as a divinely appointed priest. But the Old Testament states that you have to be a descendant of Levi to be a priest, and Jesus is indisputably descended from Levi's brother Judah (Heb 7:13-14). Not Levitical = not priest. Jesus is not Levitical, so Jesus is not a priest. That's the problem that the author of Hebrews, in his commitment to the divine authority of the Old Testament, must face. And the solution to the problem is Melchizedek. Here is a man whom the Scriptures themselves call a "priest of God Most High" (Gen 14:18) who is not from the tribe of Levi, whose priesthood is in fact superior to Levi's. And Psalm 110:4 promises that the son of David will be *that* kind of priest. There's a biblical precedent, in other words, for a non-Levitical priest.

But how do you become one of those? Not just anyone takes on that mantle. To go back to Hebrews 5 for a moment, Jesus is a Melchizedekian priest because God said so. The Father spoke Psalm 110:4 to his Son: "You are a priest forever like Melchizedek." But there's a bit more to it than that, because he has to be like Melchizedek in some way—and not in just any way but in a way that sets him apart from the Levitical priests. What do Melchizedek and Jesus have in common that could not be said of any Levite?

Indestructible Life

Jesus and Melchizedek have something in common that no one else has. Hebrews 7:16 says that Jesus became a priest "not on the basis of a legal requirement about his ancestry, but on the basis of the power of an indestructible life." In other words, physical *descent* is no longer relevant but rather physical *continuation*. That might seem an odd juxtaposition, but look at Hebrews 7:23-24. "The former priests [i.e., the Levites] were numerous because death prevented them from continuing, but he retains his priesthood permanently because he remains forever." In other words, the genealogical basis of the Levitical priesthood was tied to its greatest fault: there had to be a way to keep the priesthood going because the priests kept dying. But because Jesus never dies, his priesthood never ends. That's what connects Melchizedek and Jesus: *they never die; therefore, they never need replacing.* The Levitical priestly and sacrificial system kept having to hit the restart button, because the priests kept passing on. That problem has now gone away. "Jesus is able to save completely those who draw near to God through him, because he always lives to intercede for them" (Heb 7:25). Or in the words of the hymn, "A great high priest whose name is Love, who ever lives and pleads for me."[4]

Recap so far: Jesus is a priest, and he is a Melchizedekian priest because (1) he can't be a Levitical priest, (2) God appointed him as a Melchizedekian priest, and (3) like Melchizedek lived forever in a figurative sense, Jesus does for real. No death, no breakdown of priesthood, no cessation of ministry. Ever.

Let's pause for a moment and consider the chronology of all this. We know from Hebrews 5 that Jesus died, was raised, and then was appointed by God to be a Melchizedekian high priest. This is confirmed by what we just saw in Hebrews 7: he had to be impervious to death to be that kind of high priest, and since he died, that couldn't have been true until after the resurrection.[5] Once raised, he could never die

---

[4]"Before the Throne of God Above," lyrics by Charitie Lees Bancroft, music by Vikki Cook.
[5]Check out "Going Deeper: Christology" at the end of this book for some more reflection on how Jesus, being God, can *die, be raised (but also raise himself),* and *move from a position of mortality to a position of immortality.*

again—this is what Hebrews 11:35 calls the "better resurrection." Some women received back their loved ones via resurrection (the widow's son in 2 Kings 4:8-37, or Lazarus in Jn 11:1-44, for example), but those loved ones died again. Others refused release from torture in expectation that they would rise at the last day, never to die again—that's the better resurrection. Jesus now, us later—once raised, always raised. Jesus won't die, can't die. Death no longer has any claim on him. That is the prerequisite for his priesthood, and that is something he did not have until after his bodily resurrection. And what that implies is that *Jesus did not receive his priestly appointment, and therefore did not accomplish his priestly work of atonement, until after his resurrection.*[6]

I hope you caught that. Jesus wasn't a priest until after the resurrection. He didn't do his priestly work, therefore, until after the resurrection. He didn't offer himself as an atoning sacrifice for sins, therefore, until after the resurrection. That's what Hebrews is saying. You might be thinking, *Wait a second—isn't the cross where Jesus offered himself as an atoning sacrifice? I mean, isn't "Jesus died for my sins" about as ABCs-of-the-Christian-faith as it gets?* We've got to recognize, first of all, that "Jesus died for my sins" and "Jesus completely accomplished his sacrificial atoning work on the cross" are not the same thing. Did Jesus die for my sins? Yes. Could we not go for pages and pages merely listing, never mind explaining, all that Jesus accomplished for us on the cross? Absolutely. Does that require that everything Jesus did for me was done particularly on the cross and nowhere else? Nope.

It's rather difficult to know, in the New Testament, when we can say things like "*x* was accomplished by Jesus' death, *y* was accomplished by his resurrection, and *z* was accomplished by his ascension," and when we simply have to say "*x*, *y*, and *z* were accomplished by Jesus' life, death, resurrection, and ascension." It's tough to determine when we can parse it out and when it simply comes as a package deal. Christ died for our

---

[6]There's quite a lot of literature on this point, surprising though it may be. For a particularly well-reasoned account, see R. B. Jamieson, *Jesus' Death and Heavenly Offering in Hebrews*, Society for New Testament Studies Monograph Series 172 (Cambridge: Cambridge University Press, 2019).

sins, says Paul, but if Christ has not been raised, we are still in our sins. In that case you can't split it up like the song does: "Living, he loved me; dying, he saved me; buried he carried my sins far away; rising he justified freely forever."[7] When is this appropriate, and when is it not? I'm not sure we can always answer that question. And this is obviously an issue that concerns the whole of Scripture, not just Hebrews. But we need to let Hebrews have its moment behind the microphone before we start shouting it down just because it doesn't sound exactly like what we're used to hearing from Paul or the Gospels.

The claim that Jesus wasn't a priest (and therefore didn't do his priestly work of offering an atoning sacrifice) until after the resurrection raises two major questions. First, if he didn't offer himself on the cross, what did he do on the cross? And second, if he didn't offer himself on the cross, where did he offer himself? In the chapters that follow, I'm going to try to answer these two questions.

Study Questions

1. Read Genesis 14:17-20 and its surrounding context. What strikes you about Melchizedek's part in this story?

2. Is it odd to you that Jesus' atoning work includes, but extends beyond, the cross?

---

[7]"One Day!" lyrics by J. Wilbur Chapman, music by Charles H. Marsh.

6

JESUS THE SACRIFICE

"I'M MORE STUBBORN THAN YOU ARE." It's what I used to say to my kids when they were really little and didn't want to eat whatever we'd put in front of them. It meant, "I'm more willing to endure this situation than you are, and so you're going to have to be the one who breaks the impasse and does what I want, rather than the other way around." Three-year-olds can be pretty stubborn, and it was often my job to beat them at their own game. And so the evaluative question, meal after meal after meal: Did I permit my kids to wear me down and get their way because I just didn't want to deal with their stubbornness any longer?

God is more stubborn than we are. Or to put it another way, a way that works just as well in the parent-child situation, God is more faithful than we are. We make promises and break them. He makes promises and keeps them. If you're a parent you've probably said it this way: "I told you that if you did *x*, I was going to do *y*, and what matters most of all in this situation is that I prove myself trustworthy, because you need to know that when I say I'll do something, I'll do it." It's just a slightly more thoughtful version of "I'm more stubborn than you are." And the point is, I as a parent am going to keep my word. Of course, there are times when we say things we should never have said, and we have to own that and backtrack appropriately. But that's never the case with God. God never says, "If you don't clean your room in the next fifteen seconds, I'm going to send you to boarding school!" He says what he means, he means what he says, and that, oddly enough, is the first key to our question, If Jesus didn't offer himself as an atoning sacrifice, what *did* he do on the cross?

The End of the First Covenant

Jesus' death, according to Hebrews 9:15, "redeems those who sinned under the first covenant." How does that work? There are two covenants that God made with his people collectively. The first one is the one God made with Israel at Mount Sinai, described in Exodus 24 and in Hebrews 9:19-20. But before Hebrews describes that specific moment, the author reminds us of the general principle: "A covenant is only enforced when the person who breaks it dies" (Heb 9:17).[1] That is why "even the first covenant was not put into effect without blood" (Heb 9:18). The blood of the covenant symbolizes the penalty that rightly falls on anyone who enters into the covenant and then fails to stay faithful to it. In other words, when you signed on to the first covenant with God, you were signing your own death warrant if you broke it.

As you probably know, Israel broke it. And broke it. And broke it. And there's a long story we won't go into here of God's continued attempts to bring Israel back, to restore them, to convince them to stay faithful, and of God finally throwing up his hands and saying, "Fine— here come the curses of the covenant." Then, after judging them and sending them into exile and all that, God again reaches out and offers them a second covenant, a *new* covenant (Jer 31:31-34, which is quoted in Heb 8:8-12; 10:15-17). But Hebrews notices a problem. The problem is that the old covenant says, "Everyone who breaks this covenant has to

---

[1]Some Bibles say, "A will is in force only when somebody has died." It's a bit confusing, because the Greek word we translate "covenant" (a formal agreement made between two or more parties) is the same word that can be translated "will" (the document that distributes my belongings after I die). But in Heb 9:15 it's clearly about the Sinai covenant, and in Heb 9:18-20 it's clearly about the Sinai covenant, and the point of those verses is that covenants involve blood to show that death is the penalty for breaking the covenant. So the death mentioned in Heb 9:16-17 is most likely the death of the covenant breaker. For the details see Scott W. Hahn, "Covenant, Cult, and the Curse-of-Death: Διαθήκη in Heb 9:15-22," in *Hebrews: Contemporary Methods—New Insights*, ed. Gabriella Gelardini, Biblical Interpretation Series 75 (Leiden: Brill, 2005), 65-88.

die." But that's not what happened. Instead, Jeremiah 31:32 (quoted in Heb 8:9), describes the old covenant situation like this: "I made [the old covenant] with their ancestors when I took them by the hand to lead them out of Egypt, but they did not remain faithful to my covenant, so I disregarded them, says the LORD." Say what? They disobeyed, so God *disregarded* them? That sounds more like a parent who hears kids arguing over a toy in the other room and ignores them and hopes the situation will just resolve itself, not like a parent who has already been abundantly clear about the status of that toy and the consequences of continued conflict over it.

But this is where Jesus comes in. The old covenant is still sitting there, unfinished, because God has not yet kept his end of the bargain—to mete out proper punishment on those who disobey. But this is not because God is unfaithful, or lazy, or apathetic. It's because he is patient, because at that time (Jeremiah's time) he was preparing for the day on which he himself would live as the one Israelite who did *not* break the covenant and yet, representatively, died as the covenant breaker. Look again at Hebrews 9:15—he died in order to redeem those who sinned under the first covenant. In other words, he took on himself the penalty for breaking that covenant. If Jesus hadn't died, if God had simply moved on with a new covenant, the requirements of the first covenant would have remained unfulfilled, which means that God himself would have been a covenant breaker. He would have not fulfilled his promise to keep Israel responsible to the covenant, and he would have been as guilty as they were. So Jesus died as the recipient of the curse of the old covenant—by taking Israel's punishment (what we often call penal substitution), he redeemed them out from under the penalty that was rightly coming their way. And by doing that, he opened up the possibility of there being a new covenant between God and his people. So that's one way in which Jesus' death on the cross accomplishes atonement.

Fighting Our Fight, Winning Our Victory

Here's another way that Jesus' death was atoning. The death of Jesus, according to Hebrews, was "for everyone" (Heb 2:9). What does that mean? Keep reading. Jesus was "perfected through suffering" (Heb 2:10), and as a result "he is not ashamed to call us his siblings" (Heb 2:11). So far, then, Jesus walks the same path that we walk—a path that climaxes in death. But he is perfected in that death, not defeated by it, which means that his path diverges from ours at that point. Then he looks back at us and calls us his siblings, meaning that he took a different path from the one we inevitably take—not to separate himself from us but quite the opposite. He is the pioneer, the trailblazer, the one who takes a route you and I would not have been able to take, not to leave us behind but to bring us along with him. This is what it means, in this particular context, that his death was *for us*.

Hebrews next refers to what we call the incarnation—Jesus, the divine Son of God, taking on humanity: "Since the children [God's children, Jesus' siblings] have in common flesh-and-blood existence, he decided to join them in that so that by dying he could destroy the one who wields the power of death, that is, the devil, and free those who have always been held captive to the fear of death" (Heb 2:14-15). He takes on physicality and mortality so that, when he experiences the death that all mortal beings experience *and then overcomes it*, he sets other mortals free from the fear that inevitably enslaves anyone who sees death in their future. Jesus dies for us in the sense that his death and subsequent overcoming of death render impotent the fear of death that controls us. If death is defeated, it is no longer to be feared, nor is the one who wields it as a weapon over us. Hallelujah!

The Bloody Death of Jesus

One more thing about Jesus' death in Hebrews, and now we come back to the precise question of "In terms of Jesus' atoning sacrifice, of what significance was his death?" According to Hebrews and Leviticus, the critical item in accomplishing atonement is *blood*: "Without blood being poured out there is no forgiveness of sins" (Heb 9:22).[2] But "blood

---

[2]There is a question here as to whether "poured out" means "spilled [in death]" or "applied [in presentation]." For different perspectives see R. B. Jamieson, *Jesus' Death and Heavenly Offering in Hebrews*, Society for New Testament Studies Monograph Series 172

poured out" doesn't just mean "draw a few vials and send the animal back to pasture." Leviticus 17:11 says, "The life of the creature is in the blood. . . . It is the blood that makes atonement for one's life." The animal does have to die. Why? Because, going back to the old covenant, atonement is necessary where one's life is forfeit, and the blood is the symbol that a life has been given in exchange for that life. In other words, the presence of blood indicates that someone or something has died in place of another. Why is my life *not* owed in the form of my blood, given in death? Because Jesus' life has already been given in its place.

Jesus' death on the cross is an *important* part of the story. It just isn't the *whole* story. Hebrews tells us, first of all, that Jesus accomplished atonement by becoming a priest like Melchizedek and offering himself as a sacrifice. He can't have offered himself until he became a priest, he didn't become a priest until he had indestructible life, he didn't have indestructible life until he rose from the dead. Therefore, he didn't offer himself (and therefore accomplish atonement) until after the resurrection. But we've just seen that his lifeblood, given over in death, is what he offered. So, what gives? On to the next chapter to get some clarity.

Study Questions

1. God was faithful to his old covenant promises, though it took a while (because he's patient, not because he's slow or lazy). How have you seen God's faithfulness to his promises to you?

2. This chapter mentions three things that Jesus accomplished on the cross: substitution for sins under the old covenant, rendering death impotent, and giving up his life as the atoning sacrifice to be offered in the heavenly sanctuary. What other effects of Jesus' death can you think of?

(Cambridge: Cambridge University Press, 2019), 141-56; Michael H. Kibbe, "Is It Finished? When Did It Start? Hebrews, Priesthood, and Atonement in Biblical, Systematic, and Historical Perspective," *Journal of Theological Studies* 65 (2014): 34-35.

7

JESUS IN THE SANCTUARY

MY WIFE IS FROM NORTHERN CALIFORNIA. East of Redding, to be specific ("northern California" means different things to different people). Fire country. There was a big one in 1992, called the Fountain Fire, that started just up the hill from her family ranch. Sixty thousand acres or so, and we frequently drive by the fire line when we visit her folks. I first saw it in 2004, and two things were amazingly obvious, more than a decade later (and are still obvious to this day, after another twenty years): (1) the fire line itself, where you can see what burned and what didn't, and (2) the property lines within the burned area, where you can see which landowners were proactive in the aftermath and which ones weren't.

If you're at all aware of environmental legislation, the West Coast timber wars, conversations about climate change, and so on, you know that fires in California are ground zero for the most contentious disputes in that arena. Who did what wrong and what to do about it—don't bring this one up in public unless you're ready for some strong opinions, educated and otherwise. Don't worry, I'm not going there. Where I am going is to the fact that no one, and I mean *no one*, thinks everything is as it should be in this arena. No one thinks all is well, no one thinks nothing needs to be changed. "Do you feel the world is broken? We do."[1] We *all* do.

---

[1] Andrew Peterson, "Is He Worthy?," *Resurrection Letters: Prologue*, Centricity Music, 2018.

Hebrews has already told us that all is not yet well. Whether you read Hebrews 2:8 ("We do not yet see everything subjected to humanity") and think of war, ecological devastation, a brutal work environment, or the chaos of your own home, you think of *something, somewhere*. None of us read that phrase and think, *I don't know if I agree; I think we're actually doing a great job of stewarding God's world*. We know it's a mess. We know the world is broken, and the point is that we know *the world* is broken. Not just humans and human relationships but the space in which we and our relationships exist.

Sacred Space

We are affected by our surroundings, by the spaces in which we live. That's why, in our context of ever-increasing digital disembodiment, we've coined such terms as *safe space. Third space. Head space. Personal space*. Because *where* we live (or die) is as important as *with whom* we live (or die).

Unfortunately, a commonplace of Christian thinking is that departure from space itself, at least in the physical sense, is the goal. We think being out of place, being "in" a lifeless world, is solved by departing from material space altogether. That's wrong, so wrong, not just *not* biblical but *anti*biblical, *anti*-Christian. We know this because Hebrews 2 predicts that we are being led into glory. Not disembodied, space-less glory but the glory of those given to rule over the world to come, the new creation, where we will no longer be *ec*topic but *en*topic— we will be *in* a world that can and does nourish us and enliven us as God intended it to do. But we also know this because Hebrews 8–9 tells us that space itself needs—and receives—atonement.

> The main point of this whole conversation is that we have a high priest who sat down at the right hand of the God's throne in heaven and who ministers in the sanctuary—the true tabernacle— which was constructed by the Lord, not by a mere human. Every high priest is appointed so they can offer gifts and sacrifices, so obviously our high priest had to offer something as well. But if he were here on earth, he wouldn't be a priest, because here on earth

we already have priests who offer those gifts and sacrifices that the Law requires. (Heb 8:1-4)

You knew Hebrews was weird, right? Hebrews 7 ends by pointing out that God's oath in Psalm 110:4 ("The Lord has sworn, and will not change his mind—you are a priest forever like Melchizedek") is superior to the law, because the law appoints weak (i.e., mortal) men to the priesthood, whereas the oath "appoints a Son who has been forever perfect" (Heb 7:28). Then Hebrews 8 starts with a quick summary of all that's been said so far: that Son, that forever-perfected priest—he's *our* priest. He hasn't died, like the Levitical priests always do. He's seated right now at God's right hand, and he's still ministering on our behalf (Heb 8:1-3). And look: "If he were on earth, he wouldn't be a priest, since here on earth we already have a priestly system in place as prescribed by the law" (Heb 8:4). *If he were on earth, he wouldn't be a priest.* But he's not on earth. He's in heaven, and he's a priest there.

A Priest and a Sanctuary in Heaven

A priest in heaven? Maybe it isn't so odd at first glance. He's in the presence of God, which is kind of like being in a temple (since temples are where gods live, in theory), so that makes some sense. But for Hebrews this isn't just a general religious idea (heaven is kind of like a temple) but a concrete truth based on the Old Testament. In Hebrews 8:5, we're going to be sent back to Mount Sinai, to when Moses originally received the building instructions for the wilderness tabernacle. "When Moses was about to set up the tabernacle, he was told, 'See that you make everything according to the pattern shown to you on the mountain'" (quoting Ex 25:40). I used to picture God giving Moses some kind of blueprint—layout, dimensions, and so on. But according to Hebrews, what Moses sees isn't an architectural drawing of a temple. *It's an actual temple.*[2]

Jump ahead to Hebrews 9:11. Christ appeared as high priest not in the earthly sanctuary in the wilderness or in Jerusalem but in "the

---

[2]There is an especially helpful deep dive into this point in Benjamin J. Ribbens, *Levitical Sacrifice and Heavenly Cult in Hebrews*, Beihefte zur Zeitschrift für die neutestamentliche Wissenschaft 222 (Berlin: de Gruyter, 2016), 102-13.

greater and more perfect tent, which is not made with hands and not of this creation." Keep reading. "He entered once for all into the Most Holy Place" (Heb 9:12). Skip ahead a couple more paragraphs. "Christ has entered, not into a sanctuary made with hands (those are just copies of the real thing), but into heaven itself" (Heb 9:24). Do you see where this is going? It's not that Jesus is doing priestly work in heaven because heaven is kind of like a temple. *Heaven isn't kind of like a temple. Temples are kind of like heaven.* The sanctuary on earth (Heb 8:5) is a "shadowy illustration" of the one in heaven. If you've got a blueprint for a house, and then a house, which one is the illustration and which is the reality? But here it's not a blueprint in heaven and a reality on earth. It's the reality in heaven and a sketch drawing on earth. The sanctuary in the wilderness, the temples in Jerusalem—crude illustrations of the real thing.

This isn't fundamentally about criticizing the sanctuaries on earth. The sanctuary here and the sanctuary there have a lot in common, which shouldn't be surprising given that one is modeled on the other. And it isn't just the structure that's similar—it's the whole religious system: priests, covenants, rituals, atoning sacrifices, and sanctuaries. Hebrews 8:3, for example, says, "Every high priest is appointed to offer gifts and sacrifices—so it was necessary for this priest [i.e., Jesus] to have something to offer as well." And it's assumed that he will offer his sacrifice in a sanctuary (Heb 9:11-12), that he will offer that sacrifice in order to atone for sins (Heb 9:12), and that his offering will involve blood (Heb 9:22). The atoning work of Jesus plays by all the same rules as the atoning sacrifices mandated by God in Exodus and Leviticus—but, again, it's not because he's bound to their rules but because they are bound to his. His sanctuary came first.

A Sanctuary Cleansed in Heaven

[Moses] sprinkled the blood on the tent and all the sacred vessels. According to the law, everything is purified with blood, and without blood being poured out there is no forgiveness. So it was necessary for the copies of the heavenly things to be purified with those rituals; but the heavenly things themselves required better sacrifices. (Heb 9:21-23)

There's a sanctuary in heaven (or heaven just is a sanctuary—scholars debate this point).[3] And here are a couple of interesting things about that sanctuary. First, Hebrews 9:21-23 says that it isn't just *people* that need to be atoned for through blood sacrifice. It's the *place* as well. At-one-ment. God and creation coming together. But we have to be with God some*where*—and the *where* needs atonement just as much as the *who*. This is a tough one for those of us who have been detoxed from the very idea of sacred space, but it's an undeniable biblical fact: the space in which God and humanity come together is no less in need of purification than humanity itself.

Here's the second crazy thing: the need for sacred space (space that has been set apart and cleansed from sin's pollution) applies just as much to the sanctuary in heaven as it did to the one on earth. Just as the copies of the heavenly things—the earthly tabernacle and all the implements therein—needed to be cleansed with blood in order for that to be a suitable arena for God to be with Israel, so the heavenly things themselves needed that same cleansing (Heb 9:24). *Heaven needed cleansing just like the tabernacle did.* And how do you suppose that cleansing took place? Jesus did that when he offered himself. In heaven. As your high priest.

Think for a second, back to the previous chapter, why this might have been necessary—necessary not just in the ritual-cleansing sense but in the sense of getting done what God needs to get done to accomplish his plan. Jesus, a resurrected human being, ascends in order to reign over heaven and its angelic inhabitants—and his goal is for us to join with him in that reign. Not that we leave earth and go to heaven but that heaven comes to earth, and when we reign with Christ we do so over the creatures of heaven *and* of earth. But all this is encompassed within

---

[3]Jared Calaway, *The Sabbath and the Sanctuary: Access to God in the Letter to the Hebrews and Its Priestly Context*, Wissenschaftliche Untersuchungen zum Neuen Testament 2/349 (Tübingen: Mohr Siebeck, 2013), 105; R. B. Jamieson, *Jesus' Death and Heavenly Offering in Hebrews*, Society for New Testament Studies Monograph Series 172 (Cambridge: Cambridge University Press, 2019), 53-54.

the moment of the ascension itself—and the ascension is only second-arily about Jesus reigning over creatures. First, and fundamentally, the ascension is about God and humanity coming together. At-one-ment. Jesus enters into the presence of his Father, and *then* he takes his seat as king of heaven. And when he did that, he "prepared a place for us," as he promised the disciples he would (Jn 14:3).

Conclusion

Let's check in with where we've come so far. Jesus could not have been a high priest until he rose from the dead, because the only two options on the table are Levitical and Melchizedekian; he for sure isn't Levitical, and in order to be Melchizedekian you have to be impervious to death, which Jesus wasn't until he experienced the better resurrection. Therefore, he did not offer himself as an atoning sacrifice until after the resurrection. In addition, Hebrews points out that Jesus wouldn't have been a priest on earth anyway, because the tabernacle and temple already had priests; rather, he performed his priestly duty in heaven, where we find the original sanctuary after which the later sanctuaries were modeled. And if that makes some sense, and you'd like to know how that works and what difference that makes, it's time to move forward—backward, actually, because once more we're headed for the Old Testament. This time: Leviticus.

Study Questions

1. When you look at the world around you, what brokenness in the world comes to mind? Is it personal? Societal? Relational? Environmental? Political?

2. Is the idea of sacred space odd to you? What physical locations have you designated as sacred in various ways (places where you only dress a certain way, speak a certain way, act a certain way)?

3. Why do you suppose heaven itself needed cleansing? Do any Old Testament stories come to mind that might help us understand this?

8

JESUS AND THE DAY
OF ATONEMENT

HEBREWS USES ALL KINDS OF Old Testament sacrifices to explain various elements of what Jesus has accomplished for us. Daily sin offerings, one-time purification offerings, covenant-inauguration sacrifices, and, most importantly, the yearly ritual we call the Day of Atonement, or Yom Kippur. You might take a moment to go read Leviticus 16 to get the broad sense of things before you keep going here; some elements of that ritual are discussed in Hebrews and some aren't, but it's indisputably the most important sacrificial event for understanding what Jesus did, why he did it, where he did it, and how he got it done.[1]

Leviticus 16

Leviticus 16 is about what the high priest, and the high priest alone, does to atone for the sins of Israel. "No one else is to be in the tent from the time Aaron goes in to make atonement in the Most Holy Place until he

---

[1]R. B. Jamieson, *Jesus' Death and Heavenly Offering in Hebrews*, Society for New Testament Studies Monograph Series 172 (Cambridge: Cambridge University Press, 2019), 35-41; David M. Moffitt, *Atonement and the Logic of the Resurrection in the Epistle to the Hebrews*, Supplements to Novum Testamentum 141 (Leiden: Brill, 2011), 215-84; Gareth L. Cockerill, *The Epistle to the Hebrews*, New International Commentary on the New Testament (Grand Rapids, MI: Eerdmans, 2012), 70-72.

comes out, having made atonement for himself, his household, and for the whole community of Israel" (Lev 16:17). "The priests go regularly into the first section of the tabernacle (the 'Holy Place'), performing their cultic responsibilities, but into the second section (the 'Most Holy Place') only the high priest goes, and only once each year" (Heb 9:6-7). The Day of Atonement is the ultimate moment of human access to God. Immediately after striking down Aaron's sons for ignoring how God had arranged for the priests to have access to him, God instructs Moses, "Tell your brother Aaron that he is not to come whenever he chooses into the Most Holy Place behind the curtain in front of the mercy seat [the cover of the ark of the covenant], or else he will die, for I will appear in the cloud over the mercy seat" (Lev 16:2). Every ritual is a big deal, because they involve God and Israel getting close. The Day of Atonement is a *big deal*, because Aaron is headed all the way into God's presence, visually accessible above the ark of the covenant—and even then, the first thing he'll do when he gets in there is throw some incense on a fire so that "the smoke of the incense will conceal the mercy seat over the ark of the covenant, so that Aaron will not die" (Lev 16:13).

Leviticus 16 includes some of the most straightforward claims in the Old Testament about the need for sacred space, as well as sacred people, to be cleansed. Aaron will "sprinkle the bull's blood on the atonement cover and in front of it, and in so doing he will make atonement for the Most Holy Place because of the uncleanness and rebellion of the Israelites" (Lev 16:15-16). He will *make atonement for the Most Holy Place.* Why? *Because of the uncleanness and rebellion of the Israelites.* This is a bit of a mystery—how did the Most Holy Place come to need atonement on account of sins committed outside it? In this particular moment, the Most Holy Place was defiled by the "unauthorized fire" and subsequently scorched corpses of Nadab and Abihu, Aaron's sons (Lev 10:1-3; 16:1).[2] But the Day of Atonement was to be repeated year after year (Lev 16:34),

---

[2]L. Michael Morales, *Who Shall Ascend the Mountain of the Lord? A Biblical Theology of the Book of Leviticus,* New Studies in Biblical Theology 37 (Downers Grove, IL: IVP Academic, 2015), 145-53.

not just after someone treated God's presence as no big deal and waltzed right into his innermost sanctuary.

The problem is that impurity is contagious. It spreads like an infectious disease, but you can't quarantine yourself and ride it out. There's a phrase you'll see on occasion in Leviticus: "in your/their midst." Some Bibles will say, "among you/them." See Leviticus 15:31, which says, "You must separate the Israelites from uncleanness, so that they don't make my dwelling place *among them* unclean." Or here's an interesting one: when a dead lizard falls into a clay pot, everything "*in the midst of*" the clay pot (meaning everything that was in the pot when the dead gecko fell in) is unclean, and the pot itself must be destroyed (Lev 11:33). And in our text, Leviticus 16:16, the sanctuary needs to be atoned for because it is with them "*in the midst* of their uncleanness." You don't have to sin in the sanctuary to defile the sanctuary.

Leviticus (and the rest of the Bible, for that matter) is going to use that same phrase to describe God himself—he is "in their midst," he "dwells among them" (Ex 25:8; 29:45-46; Lev 26:11-12). But God himself can't be defiled, obviously. He can be *treated as* defiled, which is what Leviticus 10:3 implies Nadab and Abihu did. But he can't actually *be* defiled. What he can do, and what he will eventually do in the face of Israel's unrelenting impurity, is *leave* (Ezek 10:1-19; 43:1-9). He can depart from their midst. He can no longer be among them. And in order to prevent that from happening, the innermost sanctuary, the Most Holy Place, the location where God's presence is most intimately engaged, must be atoned for—must be cleansed from sin.

How does atonement happen in Leviticus 16? Blood. When and where does it happen? It doesn't happen—you might have assumed it did—when Aaron *kills* the animals. It happens when he sprinkles the blood on the mercy seat, a.k.a. the atonement cover (depending on your translation). Look again at Leviticus 16:15-16. He kills the bull outside, apparently—it doesn't actually say, but the assumption of the story is that the animal is already dead and its blood is now available for use in the ritual. But the mere fact that the animal is dead doesn't mean atonement has been accomplished. There's no atonement until the blood is applied to the mercy seat (Lev 16:15). It's a two-part ritual. *Slaughter* outside—meaning death has occurred, life has been taken in exchange for life owed, and blood has been obtained for further use. *Offering* inside—meaning the blood obtained in the exchange (a life given for a life) of the slaughter can now act as a cleansing agent whereby atonement is accomplished. The point is, *you need both*. You can't just kill an animal and call it a day. Nor can you stick a syringe into the animal, draw a few fluid ounces, and head on into the sanctuary. The animal has to die, and its blood has to then be used to accomplish the removal of sin's stain on God's people and God's sanctuary. That's how atonement works in Leviticus 16.

Leviticus 16 in Hebrews

I hope you can already see the parallels between the Day of Atonement and what Jesus did. First, he died. He can't skip that part. He can't accept the crown of thorns, draw some blood, and then whisk away to heaven. But then the other side of the coin, which is what this chapter is really all about: *just being dead outside the sanctuary isn't enough either*. Did Jesus accomplish atonement by dying on the cross? In the terms laid out by Leviticus 16 and taken up by Hebrews, *atonement* means enabling Creator and creature to come together by purifying both the creature and the space in which the reunion takes place. And if we're defining atonement that way—no. No, he didn't accomplish atonement simply by dying on the cross. He did it by dying, by rising, by ascending, and by offering himself in the heavenly sanctuary.[3] And when he did *all* that, he "accomplished purification for sins and then sat down at the right hand of the Majesty on high," as Hebrews 1:3 puts it.

Shall we unpack this a bit more? Jesus died on the cross, as the sacrificial animals died, in order to give his life in place of sinners. That's a start. But we need this sacrificial animal to come back to life. If he's dead, he can't be a priest. If he can't be a priest, he can't accomplish atonement. You

---

[3]Morales, *Who Shall Ascend?*, 167-84.

need a priest to accomplish atonement. Sure, there were priests at Jesus'
death. But they wanted him dead as a blasphemer and idolater, not as a
sacrifice. So that obviously doesn't get us anywhere. The only person
around who is qualified to present Jesus (the sacrifice) is Jesus (the priest).
So we need Jesus (the priest) to be alive. Hence, the resurrection.[4]

But even the resurrection isn't enough. We've got a sacrifice, and
we've got a priest (now that he's irrevocably alive and hence like
Melchizedek). But Leviticus 16 makes it pretty clear: you need not only
a sacrifice and a priest but a sanctuary as well. And Jesus isn't qualified
to offer himself in the temple in Jerusalem. So he needs another sanctuary, and it just so happens that there is another one—a better one, in
fact, and it's in heaven. Hence, the ascension.

Jesus arrives in heaven, having given his life on the cross. Then, as a
resurrected high priest, he heads into the presence of his Father to offer
himself as that atoning sacrifice in the heavenly sanctuary in order to
accomplish at-one-ment for both the people and the place itself. And
having done all that, the Father speaks. "You are my Son!" and so on and
so forth, and we're back to the sequence laid out in the last chapter that
climaxes with Jesus sitting at God's right hand. He sits as king of heaven—
he reigns there and will one day reign here also. But he also sits as priest
of heaven—heaven has been cleansed and made fit for God and humanity to dwell together, and the same will one day be true of earth as
well. Here's the sequence again from a few chapters back:

Create everything → take on humanity → recognize others as
future heirs → be tempted and suffer → become a high priest →
accomplish atonement → be presented to angels as Son and heir
and be invited to sit → sit → inherit everything.

Now we get to fill it in a bit more:

Create everything → take on humanity → recognize others as
future heirs → be tempted and suffer → die → rise from the dead

---

[4]Michael H. Kibbe, "'You Are a Priest Forever!' Jesus' Indestructible Life in Hebrews 7:16,"
Horizons in Biblical Theology 39 (2017): 134-55.

→ become a high priest → enter into heaven → present himself as the atoning offering in the heavenly sanctuary → be presented to angels as Son and heir and be invited to sit → sit → continue interceding for us as our high priest → inherit everything.

Every element of this story is critical. If Jesus didn't become human and do all of this as human, there's no atonement. If he died but stayed dead, there's no atonement. If there isn't any "where" that's been prepared for God and us to come together, there isn't any atonement. If Jesus isn't currently living out his vocation as our high priest, there's no atonement. It's tempting to reduce the work of Jesus to one thing or to think that affirming one part of his work is the same as denying another part. But it's not like that. God did it all because we needed it all.[5]

Study Questions

1. How does thinking about Jesus' atoning work in relation to Leviticus 16 change the way you think about what Jesus accomplished and how he accomplished it?

2. Read Genesis 3:24; 4:16; Numbers 3:38; and Leviticus 16:14. What do you notice about the pattern of movement to and away from God?

---

[5]Adam Johnson, theology professor at Biola University, likes to say that his life mission is to make the atonement bigger—meaning to expand our vision of just how much God has done for us in Christ. I think he and the author of Hebrews would have gotten along just fine.

9

FEELING OUT OF PLACE?

WHEN I WAS TWELVE YEARS OLD, my family moved from south-eastern Connecticut to Bangkok, Thailand. Being twelve already means having an identity crisis every time you look in the mirror. Now add to that moving from rural to urban (more beds in our apartment complex than in my hometown), cold to hot (winter in Bangkok means occasionally dropping below seventy-five degrees in the morning), and oh, by the way, there's the whole language and culture thing. Talk about feeling out of place. I spent the first three months hiding in my bedroom.

When I did get out, it was usually to go see something completely outside the realm of my experience. Street markets, snake farms, and, of course, Buddhist temples. Real, live temples—with monks and altars and statues and sacrifices.[1] A completely foreign experience to me, and perhaps to you as well. *Sacred space.* Incense burning and people prostrating and no way in Nirvana are we using that room for bingo night—I'm not used to this.

There's an awkwardness to thinking about being out of place in relation to the previous few chapters. The awkwardness comes from the fact that reading about priests and tabernacles and sacrifices and blood makes us feel out of place *there*, not *here*. If you've spent your life in modern North America, you might not have a frame of reference for these things. You might feel lifeless in this world, but it's not all obvious how you would be better off in that one.

---

[1]If your perception of Buddhism is meditation on a mountain and yin/yang and inner peace and all that, maybe it's worth mentioning that in Thailand Buddhism is regularly mixed in with other religious traditions such as animism and Hinduism, so sacrifices, ancestor worship, and statues of the Buddha or various deities are quite common.

I don't know that I can overcome this problem here—we would have to spend our whole lives in a cultural context that takes cultic sacred space and ritual for granted to get all the way there. But maybe it helps to notice that at the heart of it all is a sense, one that is shared even by the most rugged Western individualists, that we as humans are meant to live in healthy interaction with everything else around us. We may not know about blood purification rites, but we know about reconciliation with God and with others. We may not rely on priests, but we know about mediators, counselors, advocates, coaches, networkers. The idea of sacred space may not often cross our minds, but we know that different social contexts call for different types of clothing.

No matter our cultural context, we share with Hebrews the basic worldview that all is not right between us and God, between us and others, between us and the world, and so we are invited to share as well with Hebrews the proposal that the atoning work of Jesus as our great high priest is the definitive moment in solving those problems. But how, exactly? How does the work that Jesus has done and continues to do as priest in the sanctuary of heaven sustain my life on earth? How does his work in that world keep me alive in this world?

I think the answer lies in a crucial difference between what Aaron did in Leviticus 16 and what Jesus has done according to Hebrews 7–10. Leviticus and Hebrews agree that sin is contagious, not only from person to person but from person to place. If God is going to be with his people, and people are going to be with their God, they have to be with each other some*where*. And the *where* needs fixing just as much as the *who*.

Watch how this works in Leviticus 16. Atonement really doesn't happen, in the ritual process, until Aaron sprinkles blood on the mercy seat, in the innermost part of the sanctuary, as close to God as anyone's been since the Garden of Eden.[2] But it doesn't stop there. After the holy of holies is purified (Lev 16:14-16), Aaron starts heading back out toward the people. He purifies the outer sanctuary (the "holy place" or "tent of

---

[2] L. Michael Morales, *Who Shall Ascend the Mountain of the Lord? A Biblical Theology of the Book of Leviticus*, New Studies in Biblical Theology 37 (Downers Grove, IL: IVP Academic, 2015), 176.

meeting"; Lev 16:16), then the altar out in the sanctuary courtyard (Lev 16:18), going away from God and toward the people. Purification begins with God and ripples outward to us.

The Day of Atonement ritual ends when Aaron comes all the way back out, sends the scapegoat out into the wilderness as a sign that sin and impurity have been completely expunged from the people and the camp and the tabernacle (Lev 16:22), and offers the "Amen!" to the ceremony with the whole burnt offering (Lev 16:24).[3] The people are clean, the place is clean, and we are good to go—until next time, of course.

The first part of the ceremony maps very well onto Jesus. He provides the sacrifice by giving his life over in death on the cross and then, as resurrected high priest, enters the Most Holy Place in heaven and presents himself as the sacrifice that atones for the sins of the people and purifies the heavenly sanctuary. But then what? He sits down. He doesn't go back out, like Aaron does. He stays there.

Imagine being an Israelite on the Day of Atonement. You stand outside, waiting for Aaron to do his job. You have no idea what's going on behind the curtain. You have no idea whether Aaron's going to survive the ordeal. There really isn't anything to celebrate until Aaron emerges, unscathed, and completes the ritual. At that point, party on— but prior to that? Please hold your applause until all stages of the journey are complete.

What, then, of Jesus? He's still in there. Am I supposed to simply wait, holding my breath, hoping Jesus will come out to finish the job? Not hardly.

Remember how Hebrews starts? *God spoke.* What did he speak? Lots of things. But in this context, he spoke a promise. Hebrews calls it an *oath*. Not because other things God said are less reliable—that's the kind of oath taking Jesus tells us not to do in Matthew 5:33-37. But because he really wanted us to know how serious he was, he didn't just *say* something; he *swore it.* "God, wanting to make it even more clear to those

---

[3]Jay Sklar, *Leviticus*, Tyndale Old Testament Commentaries (Downers Grove, IL: IVP Academic, 2014), 94.

who inherit the promises how unstoppable his plan was, guaranteed it with an oath" (Heb 6:17). And what was that oath? "You are a priest *forever*, like Melchizedek." *Forever.* He won't ever stop being our priest, acting as our priest, completing his work of at-one-ment. "Jesus has a permanent priesthood. This is why he can completely save whoever comes to God through him: because he always lives to intercede for them" (Heb 7:24-25).

What are the odds that Jesus has gone into heaven and failed? What are the chances that he won't be able to finish what he started? What is the likelihood that Jesus will bail on the mission and simply stay home with his Father and leave us to die out in the cold? None whatsoever. It is as sure as the word of God itself. To whatever degree we believe that God does not lie, we can believe that our high priest is doing and will continue to do his job until he comes again for us.

If that isn't enough, we can say one more thing. Not only has Jesus successfully gone into heaven and begun the process that will climax when he returns and brings contagious purity with him, he's done one better than that: when he went into heaven, he took us with him.

Weird, right? I mean, I'm here. I'm not there. Isn't that the point? And yet Hebrews says that we can, right now, "approach God's gracious throne" (Heb 4:16). It says we can approach God now because we have already been cleansed by his blood (Heb 10:22). It says we have already come to the heavenly sanctuary along with Jesus, our priest (Heb 12:22-24).

The apostle Paul loves to say that you and I are "in Christ." Scholars use the phrase "union with Christ" to describe the same idea.[4] And while Hebrews doesn't use the Pauline phrase or the scholarly one, the idea is the same: where Jesus is, we are, because we are connected to him in some extraordinary way.

---

[4]Of the many books and essays on this topic, I have found most helpful these two: Bruce Demarest, *The Cross and Salvation*, Foundations of Evangelical Theology (Wheaton, IL: Crossway, 1997), 313-39; and Kevin J. Vanhoozer, "Wrighting the Wrongs of the Reformation? The State of the Union with Christ in St. Paul and Protestant Soteriology," in *Jesus, Paul, the People of God and N. T. Wright*, ed. Nicholas Perrin and Richard B. Hays (Downers Grove, IL: IVP Academic, 2011), 234-61.

If you dig into more technical conversations about union with Christ, you won't have to look hard to find the word *mysterious*.[5] It's not obvious at all what it means for you or me to be "in" Christ—that's just not a way of talking that maps comfortably onto how we describe other relationships. The Bible never really defines what it means to be "in Christ," but it does give us a bunch of analogies for it. We are connected to Christ like a body is connected to a head (Rom 12:4-5), like a branch is connected to a vine (Jn 15:1-17), like a wife is connected to a husband (Eph 5:23-32). Each of these analogies says something different about what it means for us to be "in Christ," even though none of them gives what we might think of as a straightforward definition of the idea.

In Hebrews, union with Christ means a couple of things. Ultimately, it means we will reign with Christ in the new creation when all things are redeemed and at-one-ment is complete. Because we are united to him as siblings, when he inherits everything (Heb 1:2), we inherit along with him (Heb 1:14; 2:5). Right now, though, it means that we are able to do certain things that Jesus has done and is doing.

Because Jesus kept his eyes on the prize and has already prepared a place for us (Heb 12:2), we are able to persevere by faith until the moment of completion—rejecting the temptation to derive pleasure from apathy (Heb 3:6).

Because Jesus suffered and died (Heb 2:9, 14), we are able to suffer— rejecting the temptation to find satisfaction in comfort (Heb 13:12-13).

Because Jesus lowered himself to become like us so he could sympathize with us as our high priest (Heb 4:14-16), we are able to love—rejecting the temptation to receive life through selfishness (Heb 13:1).

Because Jesus has been announced as the Son and enthroned with his Father (Heb 1:3), we are able to speak with our Father as his beloved children—rejecting the temptation to ground our identity in autonomy (Heb 10:21-22).

Apathy and comfort and selfishness and autonomy: attractive and available though they might be, they are Dead Sea fruit, turning to ash

---

[5]For example, Demarest, *Cross and Salvation*, 333.

in our mouths.[6] They cannot sustain us. They will not satisfy us. And yet we live, we are sustained, we are *located* in Christ, our great high priest who sits with his Father in the purified heavenly sanctuary and invites us to commune with him there even while we endure here.

Study Questions

1. Is the term "union with Christ" a familiar one to you? In what contexts have you heard it used, if any?

2. Consider the analogies that the New Testament gives for union with Christ: a body and a head (Romans 12:4-5), a branch and a vine (John 15:1-17), and a wife and a husband (Ephesians 5:23-32). What do you learn about our relationship to Christ from each of these?

3. C. S. Forester used the image of a "Dead Sea fruit that turned to ashes in the mouth." What sorts of things have you treated as life giving that turned out like that?

---

[6]C. S. Forester, *Flying Colors* (New York: Little, Brown, 1938), 243.

SECTION 3

JESUS' INVITATION INTO LIFE

MY WIFE, ANNIE, AND HER BROTHERS once made the mistake, at some point in junior high or high school, of telling their dad that "history is boring." Not the sort of thing you say to my father-in-law, who—in order to impress on his kids the beauty and value of history—signed the whole family up with the local chapter of the Reenactors of the American Civil War.

Fast-forward ten years. Dad is the commanding officer of the Union regiment, and the kids (now adults) are donning their period-appropriate attire and heading out to war. They're getting ready for the Mc-Cloud River Railroad Reenactment, a yearly event in which they've participated numerous times, but this time they're joined by a future member of the clan: me. I'd arrived in California only a couple of weeks earlier, having relocated there to pursue Annie, and this (in hindsight) was one of their "welcome to the family—let's see whether you can hack it" scenarios. Heavy wool uniform, metal canteen, canvas tent, single-shot Sharps .50 caliber rifle, and, for my unit, a couple of hours in triple-digit heat marching around the hills of northern California looking for the boys and girls in gray.

I learned a lot that day that turned out to be useful in my developing relationship with Annie and her family. But I also noticed something that turns out to be useful for understanding my out-of-placeness in the world (not just in an 1860s Army uniform). I noticed that there's a difference between a *retelling*, on the one hand, a *redo*, on the other, and a *reenactment* in the middle between the two. A *retelling*, like the Ken Burns Civil War documentary or the movie *Gods and Generals*, says, "This moment remains interesting." A *redo*, which in this case would mean South Carolina trying to bring back African American slavery and secede from the Union again, says, "This moment remains *unfinished.*"[1] But a *reenactment*, which is what we did on the slopes of Mount Shasta that day back in 2005, says, "This moment remains *crucial*—we aren't who we are without this moment."

Did you know that there's an entire book in the Bible built around the concept of a reenactment? Two books, actually. The second one is Hebrews, but that's not where the idea came from. Hebrews got it from Deuteronomy. Deuteronomy is, at its core, a *covenant reenactment ceremony*. But before we look at the Deuteronomic ceremony, it's worth asking why a covenant reenactment ceremony would be worth having in the first place.

Covenants with God are our source of life. There's a lot of fine print, obviously, but the simple fact is that you and I exist only because God considers our existence worthwhile. If you take *God* out of the equation, you take *life* out of it as well. And not just biological life—life in the sense of purpose, meaning, value, enjoyment, fulfillment. This is what God offers to us when he invites us into covenant relationship with him.

It was once the case that we received that life by being with God in his creation, in the Garden of Eden. But our rejection of that life meant that God's life could not trickle down from us to the rest of his creation, or from the rest of his creation to us. And so the very space in which we live died and became a source of death for us as well. And yet God desires to give us life, he continues to offer us life, and so he offers these things we call covenants. His side of these covenants has two parts: that he will bring us once again into the fullness of life and that he will keep us alive until that day. Our side is the mirror image of these: that we would seek life where it may be found and that we would trust him to keep us alive

---

[1] This applies as well to Confederate flag–waving, War of Northern Aggression–protesting White supremacists—it's not a reenactment if you're trying to *undo* the effects of a pivotal event.

until we find it. But we are forgetful, we are troubled, we are lazy, we are distracted, we are assaulted—so much about our current form of existence is designed to facilitate covenant faith*less*ness, and so we need covenant reenactments to keep us alive. How so? A couple of ways.

First, covenants define loyalties. I can have only one spouse. "They shall become one flesh" (Gen 2:24). I can have only one God. "As for me and my house, we will serve the Lord" (Josh 24:15). A covenantal relationship is by definition exclusive. And when Adam and Eve decided they wanted options, decided they wanted to put both good and evil on the table and choose between the two, they did what we all do, which is naturally to revolt against any sort of exclusive commitment. Not every relationship is exclusive, of course—I can have more than one friend, more than one child, more than one job. But some relationships are covenantal precisely because they are exclusive, and there's something in me that doesn't want to color inside those lines, and that is why I need reenactments. I need reminders, but not just "Hey, remember that promise you made to your wife" kinds of reminders. I need something physical, something tangible, something that puts me physically back in the covenantal moment.[2] Reenactment sustains loyalty far better than mere reminder.

Another reason we need covenant reenactments is that covenants define expectations. "Worship Yahweh your God and serve him only" is the fundamental expectation of God's covenant with Israel—that's the exclusive-loyalty part. But Israel signed up for a lot more specificity than that when they agreed to their covenant with God. Israel saying, "We know we're keeping the covenant because we're not bowing down to Zeus," would be like saying, "I know I'm keeping the marriage covenant because I'm not sleeping with anyone else." Turns out it's a bit more complicated than that. A retelling can throw all those details at me, but I won't remember them.

A third reason we need reenactments is that covenants define identity. I mean that in a couple of different ways. One is that human identity

---

[2]Hint: marriage has one of these. See "Love and Marriage" in chapter sixteen of this book.

necessarily involves the whole human person. Anything involving my identity involves *me*—all of me, not just part of me. If my body belongs to Annie but not my mind or my emotions, that's not good enough. The covenant is between Annie and me, not between part of her and part of me. Likewise, a reenactment involves all of me in a way that a retelling doesn't. Sleeping on the ground. Drinking from that metal canteen. Smelling gunpowder. Hearing and feeling the cannons erupt. Sweating in a way I've forgotten how to do with all my moisture-wicking workout attire. The involvement of all five senses, whether in comfortable or uncomfortable ways, reminds me of who *I* am as a citizen of the United States in the aftermath of the 1860s.

The other way covenant reenactments reinforce identity is that they remind us, as parents so often remind their children, to "remember who you are no matter where you are." I spent my junior high and high school years in Thailand. Still an American citizen. Most weekdays I drive away from my house and spend the next eight hours or so in an office. Still Annie's husband. As God's much-loved children, we are—there's that word again—ectopic. Out of place. We're not home yet. But we are still his children, still in covenant relationship with him. Like being American in Thailand or Annie's husband at work, the question becomes, How do we live as covenant partners with God while we are, in a certain sense, absent from him? How do we be who we are no matter where we are—especially when where we are is not where we need to be?

All that to say—if *covenant* is the right word for our relationship with God, then reenactment is the right pathway to staying faithful to that covenant, especially when we are pursuing life within a world that cannot give it to us. What does that look like, biblically speaking? Cue Deuteronomy.

10

DEUTERONOMY

IN EXODUS 19, ISRAEL ARRIVED AT MOUNT SINAI. They stayed there through the end of Exodus, all of Leviticus, and several chapters into Numbers. When they left the mountain in Numbers 9–10, they traveled to Kadesh and prepared to enter their new land (Num 13). But they wimped out and wouldn't enter, so God sent them back to the wilderness until the adult generation died out (Num 14).

Forty years later, when they came to the east side of the Jordan River for a second try at taking the land, all the men and women who had witnessed God's presence at Sinai and signed on to the covenant with him there had died. But God's words (both directly and through Moses) at Sinai told Israel everything they needed to know about how to live life in the land, so it just wasn't going to work to send in an Israelite generation that hadn't been—or at least hadn't been adults—at Sinai. Imagine going through premarital counseling with one person but then marrying someone else. Actually, in this case, it would be more like going through the marriage *ceremony* with one person but then moving forward in life with someone else. Not a good plan. So when that crowd of Israelites gathered in front of Moses to get instructions on taking and keeping the land, there was a problem. Moses couldn't just *retell* the Sinai story—"Hey, remember when God invited us to be his people and promised to give us this land?" They didn't remember, because they weren't there. He had to *reenact* it.[1]

As you read Deuteronomy, you'll find no hint that the earth shook like it had at Sinai or that God audibly spoke to that generation like he had to their parents and grandparents on the mountain. That's because, like I said earlier, a reenactment stands somewhere between a retelling and a redo. A redo says, "Let's walk back to the mountain, literally, and try this again, because it didn't work the first time." A retelling says, "Isn't it interesting how that happened way back then?" A reenactment says, "What happened in the past is so vital to our understanding of the present that those who weren't there the first time need to relive the moment."

This unfolds in Deuteronomy in several different ways. First, Moses treats his audience as though they actually had been at Sinai (Deuteronomy calls it Horeb, but it's the same place): "Remember the day *you* stood before Yahweh your God at Horeb!" (Deut 4:10). "Yahweh spoke with *you* face to face out of the fire on the mountain" (Deut 5:4).

Second, he tells them that the covenant set up at Horeb isn't a thing of the past but of the present. "Yahweh our God made a covenant with us at Horeb. He didn't make that covenant with our ancestors, but with us—all of us who are alive here today!" (Deut 5:2-3).

Third, Moses loves the word *today* (over seventy times in Deuteronomy). You can imagine someone standing there listening, thinking, *Of course it's today—what other day would it be?* But when his words were read, over and over and over in the years and centuries to come, *today* didn't get changed to "back then." It's *always* today (that is, the day when God confirmed his covenant with the people) when Deuteronomy is read.[2]

Fourth, continued reenactment is not a happenstance. It's not as though you find yourself randomly reading Deuteronomy and think,

---

[1]Michael H. Kibbe, *Godly Fear or Ungodly Failure? Hebrews 12 and the Sinai Theophanies*, Beihefte zur Zeitschrift für die neutestamentliche Wissenschaft 216 (Berlin: de Gruyter, 2016), 53-64.

[2]There's an interesting connection here to Heb 3:13; 4:7, where the word *today* in Ps 95 is the key to understanding that the promise made to Israel in the wilderness is still available to us.

Hey, this is interesting, it's like I'm on Mount Sinai. Moses *commands* them to read it, out loud, to the whole community, at regular intervals (Deut 31:9-13). He commands them to repeat its instructions incessantly: "Teach them diligently to your children. Discuss them while you sit at home and while you are out walking along the road, when you lie down and when you get up. Bind them around your hands and on your foreheads as symbols. Write them on the doorposts of your houses and on your gates" (Deut 6:7-9). The reenactment happens formally every seven years but informally *all the time.* The call to covenant faithfulness should never be silenced.

And what if it is silenced? What happens if the reenactors take their Torah and go home? What happens if the Word of God is not read as it should be? Moses is not vague on this point: "If you do not obey Yahweh your God and keep all the instructions I am giving you today, all these curses will come on you" (Deut 28:15). And the remainder of Deuteronomy 28 is so horrific in its description of the judgment of God on disobedient Israel that I hesitate to put it in print here. Here's a sampling:

> Because of the suffering your enemy will inflict on you during the siege, you will eat the fruit of the womb, the flesh of the sons and daughters the Lord your God has given you. Even the most gentle and sensitive man among you will have no compassion on his own brother or the wife he loves or his surviving children, and he will not give to one of them any of the flesh of his children that he is eating. It will be all he has left because of the suffering your enemy will inflict on you during the siege of all your cities. The most gentle and sensitive woman among you—so sensitive and gentle that she would not venture to touch the ground with the sole of her foot—will begrudge the husband she loves and her own son or daughter the afterbirth from her womb and the children she bears. For in her dire need she intends to eat them secretly because of the suffering your enemy will inflict on you during the siege of your cities. (Deut 28:53-57 NIV)

I'll just leave that there for a moment so you can process it. That's really nasty. Think God takes covenant faithfulness seriously? "I have set before you life and death, blessings and curses. Now choose life" (Deut 30:19). *Choose life.* Choose life, because you're really not going to like the alternative.[3]

Perhaps the intensity of that paragraph from Deuteronomy is tempered by the idea that "God just isn't like that anymore." I mean, maybe God used to bring down judgment and curses and wrath and all that, but surely *our* God wouldn't do such a thing. We'll get into the details in the next few chapters, but I need to warn you now. Go back to the first sentence of Hebrews. "God spoke to us." Which God? The same God who spoke to our ancestors through the prophets (that includes Deuteronomy, by the way). The same God who spoke Deuteronomy 28 has now spoken to us in his Son. And, as it turns out, he hasn't changed a bit.

Study Questions

1. Have you ever watched or participated in a reenactment? How did that experience enable you to be affected by an event that happened a long time ago?

2. Deuteronomy has a lot to say about what God's like when he's angry, but also a lot about his overwhelming love for his people. God's righteousness and God's love can be hard for us to hold together—we tend to think of him as either always nice or always angry. Do you tend to think of God as primarily one or the other?

---

[3]J. Gary Millar, *Now Choose Life: Theology and Ethics in Deuteronomy*, New Studies in Biblical Theology (Grand Rapids, MI: Eerdmans, 1998).

11

DEUTERONOMY
AND HEBREWS

COVENANT REENACTMENTS, COVENANT FAITHFULNESS, covenant consequences. They're in Deuteronomy—but what about Hebrews? Check out this sampling of thematic connections between Deuteronomy and Hebrews:[1]

- Both are sermons written to groups of God's people at the crossroads of faithfulness and apostasy.

- Both switch constantly between telling of God's own faithfulness and summoning the audience to "go and do likewise," as Jesus puts it, as well as between warning and encouragement—positive and negative reinforcement get equal billing in both books.

- Both use Israel's refusal to press forward into the land at Kadesh Barnea as the prototype of what *not* to do (Deut 1:19-46; Heb 3:7–4:7).

- Both acknowledge that life has been hard but insist that such hardship is the maker of true sonship and should motivate perseverance rather than laziness (Deut 8:1-5; Heb 12:5-17).

---

[1]Deeper analysis of the correspondence between Deuteronomy and Hebrews appears in Michael H. Kibbe, *Godly Fear or Ungodly Failure? Hebrews 12 and the Sinai Theophanies*, Beihefte zur Zeitschrift für die neutestamentliche Wissenschaft 216 (Berlin: de Gruyter, 2016), 120-34; David M. Allen, *Deuteronomy and Exhortation in Hebrews: A Study in Narrative Re-presentation*, Wissenschaftliche Untersuchungen zum Neuen Testament 2/238 (Tübingen: Mohr Siebeck, 2008), 44-223.

- Both call "today" the day of God's appearing to them and therefore the day to respond to that appearance (Deut 5:1-3; Heb 3:7–4:11).

- Both audiences are given the opportunity to obediently press forward into God's "rest" or else forfeit the promised blessings and instead fall under a curse (Deut 11:26-32; 30:15-18; Heb 6:7-8).

- Both audiences are depicted as standing simultaneously at the mountain and at the threshold of the Promised Land (Deut 4:10-12; Heb 4:11-13; 12:22-24).

- Both audiences hear God speak from the mountain and must either accept his word in faith or reject it in disobedience (Deut 28:1-2, 15; Heb 4:1-2; 12:18-24).

- Both audiences are called to leave "Moses" behind and move ahead under the leadership of "Joshua" (in Greek the names Jesus and Joshua are the same; Deut 31:1-8; 34:8-9; Heb 3:1-6).

- Both are called to look back to the establishment of their covenant with God to ensure their continued commitment to it (Deut 18:15-18; 31:9-13; 32:47; Heb 12:22-29).

I hope this list makes it clear that, in terms of what they are trying to accomplish and how they go about accomplishing it, Hebrews and Deuteronomy are *really* similar. Chances are, Hebrews is imitating Deuteronomy (something quite a lot of people did in Hebrews' day), but just sharing a bunch of rhetorical and stylistic features isn't quite enough to prove that point. Coincidences happen. But if Hebrews were to not only look like Deuteronomy but actually *use* Deuteronomy, that might be a bit more convincing, wouldn't it? Here's a list of some of the places where Hebrews either quotes (uses the exact same words) or alludes (uses very similar language and/or concepts) to Deuteronomy:

Hebrews 1:6 // Deuteronomy 32:43

Hebrews 2:1 // Deuteronomy 4:9, 15, 23

Hebrews 2:2 // Deuteronomy 33:2

Hebrews 2:4 // Deuteronomy 4:34

Hebrews 6:7-8 // Deuteronomy 11:11-28, 29:23-24

Hebrews 10:23 // Deuteronomy 32:4

Hebrews 10:25 // Deuteronomy 32:35

Hebrews 10:27 // Deuteronomy 29:20

Hebrews 10:28 // Deuteronomy 17:6

Hebrews 10:30 // Deuteronomy 32:35-36

Hebrews 12:1-2 // Deuteronomy 20:4

Hebrews 12:3 // Deuteronomy 20:3

Hebrews 12:5-6 // Deuteronomy 8:5

Hebrews 12:15 // Deuteronomy 29:17

Hebrews 12:18-19 // Deuteronomy 5:22-25

Hebrews 12:21 // Deuteronomy 9:19

Hebrews 12:29 // Deuteronomy 4:24

Hebrews 13:6 // Deuteronomy 31:6

That's quite a list! It's a longer list than you'll find between Hebrews and any other Old Testament book, except maybe Psalms, since Psalm 110 is so common in Hebrews. Notice a couple of things before we get into the details. First, there's a little bit of Deuteronomy in the early chapters of Hebrews and a *lot* of Deuteronomy in the later chapters of Hebrews. Deuteronomy gets more important the further we go in Hebrews.

Second, Deuteronomy connections tend to clump in what we call the warning passages (Heb 2:1-4; 3:7–4:11; 6:1-8; 10:19-39; 12:18-29). There aren't any specific word connections to Deuteronomy in the second warning passage (Heb 3:7–4:11), other than *today*, but if you go back to the list of rhetorical similarities between the two books you'll see a lot of references to that part of Hebrews there.

Third, Deuteronomy 32 makes quite a few appearances. That portion of Deuteronomy is a song that God gave to Moses to give to Israel (Deut 31:19, 30), and at the end of the song he says, "These aren't just idle words for you—they are your life!" (Deut 32:47). A song to recall God's faithfulness and their covenant with him (one scholar calls it "Israel's national anthem") seems like a good idea, right up until God calls it a "witness *against* Israel" because of their inevitable unfaithfulness (Deut 31:19-21).[2] And the point is that in later generations, they're supposed to sing lines such as, "They [*the Israelites themselves—the very people singing the song!*] are a nation without sense, there is no discernment in them" (Deut 32:28) and, "Yahweh rejected them because he was angered by his sons and daughters" (Deut 32:19). Imagine singing *that* before the big game. The song is really a public self-indictment, a perpetual admission of their failure and God's faithfulness. Hebrews is obeying Moses' command to keep the song front and center in worship, and at the same time keeping its audience mindful of the fact that their covenant God is not to be trifled with.

Third, you'll discover as you read these portions of Hebrews that *none* of them say anything critical about the old covenant. We often think of Deuteronomy as precisely what went wrong in that relationship: God gave a bunch of rules, but Israel didn't keep them, so God had to come with a plan B (Jesus). But wherever that way of thinking about Deuteronomy comes from, it certainly doesn't come from Hebrews. For Hebrews, the point of leaning so heavily on Deuteronomy is not to point out what's *different* between then and now but quite the opposite. The God who established a covenant relationship with Israel on the terms laid out in Deuteronomy is the same God who has established a covenant relationship with us on the terms laid out in Hebrews—and it just so happens that those terms are nearly identical in both instances. And when they are different, the difference is the opposite of what you might expect.

God Hasn't Changed (Hebrews 10:26-31)

You can see from the list a couple of pages back that Hebrews has a little bit of Deuteronomy in the early chapters, but it's in Hebrews 10 and Hebrews 12 that the connections start showing up everywhere. Here's one of the key sections, Hebrews 10:26-31:

---

[2]Daniel I. Block, "The Power of Song: Reflections on Ancient Israel's National Anthem," in *How I Love Your Torah, O LORD! Studies in the Book of Deuteronomy* (Eugene, OR: Cascade, 2011), 162-88.

> If we keep on deliberately sinning after we receive the knowledge
> of the truth, there no longer remains any sacrifice for sins, but
> rather a terrifying expectation of judgment and a zealous fire that
> will consume God's enemies. Anyone who ignores the law of
> Moses died without mercy on the testimony of two or three wit-
> nesses. How much more severely should the one be punished who
> tramples on the Son of God, treats as unholy the blood of the
> covenant that made them holy, and insults the Spirit of grace? For
> we know the one who said, "Vengeance is mine—I will repay," and
> again, "The Lord will judge his people." It is a terrifying thing to
> fall into the hands of the living God!

This feels old-fashioned, doesn't it? It sounds like the sort of thing the
mean Old Testament God might have said way back then to Israel—but
surely not now and surely not to us. But look: "If *we* deliberately keep
on sinning . . ." Banish from your mind any thought that the anger of
God displayed in Deuteronomy could never be directed at you, no
matter how blatantly you might reject him.

The Deuteronomic nature of this paragraph starts with God's dis-
pleasure against the covenant breaker: they will face a "zealous fire that
is about to consume those who oppose God" (see Deut 29:19-20 for a
close parallel). A comparison follows between Deuteronomy's instructions about consequences for disobedience and those that apparently
are in place now. If two or three witnesses testify that you rejected God's
word through Moses, you die (Deut 17:6), but *how much worse off* will
the person be against whom the Son of God, the blood of the covenant,
and the Spirit of grace testify. Everything that makes the new covenant
better than the old covenant also makes the consequences of rejecting
the new covenant worse than the consequences of rejecting the old covenant. Remember the curses of Deuteronomy 28? Worse than that.

Think God has eased up on being a righteous judge? Don't kid
yourself: "We know," Hebrews says, "the God of Deuteronomy." The God
who said, "Vengeance is mine—I will repay" (a direct quote of Deut
32:35). *That* God hasn't changed. If you reject the mediator of your

covenant relationship with God, if you reject the blood that purified you so that you could enter into that relationship, if you reject the Spirit who calls you into that relationship and enables you to live according to its requirements, what do you expect? "The Lord *will* judge his people" (a direct quote of Deut 32:36). The last sentence of the text, describing God in the same terms found in Deuteronomy 5:26, is almost unnecessary: "It is a terrifying thing to fall into the hands of the living God." You think?

Coming Even Closer (Hebrews 12:18-29)

The climax of Hebrews is a contrast between two mountains: Sinai (it isn't named, but all the descriptions in Heb 12:18-21 come directly from the accounts of Israel's experience there in Exodus and Deuteronomy) and Zion (not the one in Jerusalem but the one in heaven).

> You have not come to a mountain that can be touched, to burning fire, to darkness, to gloom, to storm, to trumpet blast, to sounds such that those who heard the words refused to hear any more of them—since they couldn't handle the command, "If even an animal touches the mountain, let it be stoned." That scene was so terrifying that Moses himself said, "I am fearful and trembling." No, you have come to Mount Zion, to the city of the living God, to the heavenly Jerusalem, to countless angels gathered in celebration, to the church of the firstborn whose names are written in heaven, to God the Judge of all, to the spirits of the perfected righteous, to the mediator of the new covenant (Jesus), to the sprinkled blood that speaks better than Abel. (Heb 12:18-24)

If any portion of Hebrews could make you say, "See—God used to be scary, but now he's not!" it's this one. Not a mountain full of darkness and earthquakes and death sentences but party central: angels and redeemed humanity in full festival mode around the throne of God in heaven. Little wonder this text is often portrayed as "fear" (= Old Testament) versus "joy" (= New Testament).[3] And there must be some

[3]Richard T. France, "A Tale of Two Mountains: Mountains in Biblical Spirituality," *Rural Theology* 6, no. 2 (2008): 122.

truth to that—clearly being with God on the heavenly Mount Zion is designed to be a more pleasant experience than Israel's encounter with him on Mount Sinai.

But wait just a moment. That isn't the whole picture, not if Deuteronomy has anything to say about it. Look at the final bit of this text, the absolute climax of the whole book of Hebrews: "Since we are receiving an unshakable kingdom, let us give thanks, and in doing so offer acceptable worship to God with reverent awe, because our God is a consuming fire" (Heb 12:28-29).[4] Celebrate our welcome into God's heavenly dwelling? Absolutely! Breathe a deep sigh of relief because God doesn't have to be taken seriously anymore? Not a chance. The last phrase is a direct quote of Deuteronomy 4:24—God is a "consuming fire." Not a "soon all those around can warm up in its glowing" fire, not a "painful but it's good for you" fire. A *consuming* fire—remember Nadab and Abihu, back in Leviticus 10? A "don't mess with a holy God" fire. Now this is a bit confusing, because the overarching emphasis of this portion of Hebrews is difference (we have not come to Israel's *mountain*) but the climax is similarity (we have come to Israel's *God*).

To understand why coming to Mount Zion would be both cause for celebration and cause for "reverent awe," we need to go back to Mount Sinai. In Exodus 19, God came to Sinai in the presence of the whole nation of Israel, and the results were predictable: in the face of fire, darkness, earthquakes, and all the rest, Israel panicked.[5] "Yeah, about that whole direct-contact-with-God thing"—they said to Moses—"why don't you just take care of that yourself and fill us in later, because we're out of here" (Ex 20:18-19).[6]

Israel's request that Moses stand between them and God had a positive outcome and a negative one. The positive outcome was that Israel

---

[4]William L. Lane, *Hebrews 9–13*, Word Biblical Commentary 47B (Dallas: Word, 1991), 489; Barnabas Lindars, "The Rhetorical Structure of Hebrews," *New Testament Studies* 35 (1989): 402.

[5]If you want to get a sense of the scene, google "dirty thunderstorm" and look at the pictures.

[6]This scene in Ex 19–20, and its unpacking in Deut 4–5 and Heb 12, is the subject of my book *Godly Fear or Ungodly Failure?*

had a mediator: someone who could keep the lines of communication open between them and God, someone who could beg God for mercy when Israel decided a couple of weeks later to break the covenant and worship another god (Ex 32–34). But the negative outcome was that distance was established as the norm: Moses would always stand between Israel and its God. In a business deal, that sort of mediation works just fine: someone brokers the deal between my company and yours, and no one cares whether you and I ever meet face to face. But in a covenant relationship? Imagine a marriage counselor who never put husband and wife in a room together but always kept them separate and relayed messages back and forth between the two for the rest of their lives.

So Israel is kept separate from God, to some degree. Considering their sinfulness, that's not such a bad thing. But now there's a new mediator in town, Jesus, and he's going to do things differently. Notice how the descriptions of the mountains each conclude with a description of the mediator: you have not come to Moses, who is just as terrified as everyone else (Heb 12:21), but you have come to Jesus, the mediator of the new covenant, and his blood (Heb 12:24). Moses stands trembling on the mountain, feet in the presence of the Almighty but heart wishing he were back in the camp with everyone else. Jesus sits confidently at God's right hand, his hand stretched out to yours, calling you to join him. Moses can't bring you with him and, deep down, he would rather not be there himself at this particular moment. Jesus, on the other hand, has the confidence not only to be with God himself but to bring you along with him.

With unhindered access comes clarity. Sinai was a mysterious place: hard to see on account of the darkness, hard to hear on account of the noise, hard to think on account of your fear. Zion brings clarity: God is *there*, along with Jesus and the angels and the departed saints. No clouds, no darkness, no storms. Ah—but such a vision should not only fill your soul with joy but bring you to your knees. You are *in the presence of God.* Jesus isn't going up and down the mountain, relaying messages back and forth and keeping you at a safe distance from the fire. You're right there with him. God is just as big as he was at Sinai, and the only thing that's changed is that you're closer to him than Israel ever was.

Jesus adamantly refuses to go back and forth between us and God, keeping us at arm's length from each other. He's far too good a mediator—better than Moses was!—for that. Jesus' job is to get us in close. So come carefully, come respectfully, but do come. To do otherwise is to reject the adequacy of the mediator—to claim that Jesus has either failed to make it desirable, or failed to make it possible, for us to stand with his Father as his siblings. If the promises of Hebrews 1–2 don't appeal to you (come rule over all the new creation as a child of God), or if the accomplishments of Hebrews 5–10 don't satisfy you (your sins are atoned for, so come on in!), there's not much more to be said. For you, little else remains but "a terrifying expectation of judgment and a zealous fire that will consume God's enemies" (Heb 10:27).

Study Questions

1. Read Deuteronomy 32, sometimes called "The Song of Moses." What do you imagine it was like to sing that song over and over with the Israelite community?

2. Do you tend to think that God has changed—that he used to be mean, but now he's nice? How does your reading of Deuteronomy and other parts of the Old Testament change if you assume that he's the same God then and now?

3. Does it intimidate you to think about coming near to God when you think about him as a "consuming fire"?

12

THE PRESENCE OF GOD

ISRAEL IN THE WILDERNESS lived in tension. They had entered into covenant relationship with God. But they hadn't entered into the land. And remember from the last section that being *with* God means being with him some*where*. They had their *who* but not their *where*. A big part of why we have Deuteronomy in the first place is that covenant reenactments keep us on track, keep us alive, as we journey toward the *where*.

As it turns out, even living in Canaan, the Promised Land, wasn't the last word on the *where* of Israel's life with God. Hebrews 4 tells us that their final rest didn't happen then, even up through the time of David, because God's ultimate invitation was not to enter Canaan but to enter the new creation. That generation who heard Moses conduct the reenactment did enter the land, but the fullness of life with their God did not await them. Joshua, Judges, Ruth, Samuel, Kings, Chronicles—this portion of the Bible begins Israel with going into the land and ends with Israel leaving it (just like Deuteronomy said they would)—clearly that wasn't the grand finale.[1]

Here's the point: Israel conducted its first covenant reenactment just outside the land, but they were told to keep on conducting them

---

[1]Scholars use the phrase "Deuteronomistic History" to describe what we call the Historical Books in order to highlight that they are all in various ways telling the story of Israel's history within the framework of their obedience or disobedience to the commands given in Deuteronomy.

perpetually once inside the land. Continued reenactment was necessary because they were still ectopic, because neither they nor the land had been brought into complete life with God. And that continued reenactment had two components: "every moment holy" kinds of occasions (walking, standing, sitting, talking, eating) and special occasions where the whole nation came together, read the words of Deuteronomy, and relived the covenant-making moment on the mountain.[2]

Now, we have what Hebrews—borrowing from Jeremiah—calls a new covenant. It too has an inauguration moment wherein God has offered us life and we have accepted it. And it too has reenactments in which covenant partners come together and—wait. *Come together.* That's the point, right? That God would be *with* us, and we would be *with* him? We're still out of place, still waiting for the final consummation. But we are not alone. He is with us. That is why we live, even when we are out of place. But what does that mean? How does that work? That is, how do we be with God and therefore receive life from him via covenant reenactment *now*? The old covenant had both informal and formal reenactments. What about the new covenant?

I think the answer to this lies in how Hebrews invites us to be *with* God—but it's fair to ask at this point what exactly it means, on Hebrews' terms, to be with God or, as we often say, "in the presence of God." That's a phrase we use in a lot of different ways, as does the Bible itself. Psalm 139 questions whether we could ever *not* be in God's presence. In Exodus 19, Israel experienced God's presence on the mountain in all kinds of atmospheric disturbances (wind, fire, earthquake, etc.), while in 1 Kings 19 Elijah experienced the same thing at the same place as precisely none of those things—for him God was not in the storm but rather in the silence after the storm. Jesus said that to be with him was to be with the Father. So what does it look like for us? Hebrews isn't going to give us the whole answer to that question, but it does say a few things that turn out to be pretty helpful when it comes to life in a lifeless world.

---

[2] If you're not familiar with the Every Moment Holy series by Douglas McKelvey, I highly recommend it.

God's Presence and Prayer

The first way that we are with God, and therefore receive life from him, is through prayer. Some of the most well-known verses in Hebrews say this:

> Since we have a great high priest (Jesus the Son of God) who has ascended into heaven, let's hold on tightly to our confession of faith. We don't have a high priest who is unable to sympathize with our weaknesses, but one who has been tempted in every way, just like we have, but he never responded to that temptation by sinning. So let's approach God's throne of grace with boldness so that we can receive mercy and find grace when we need it. (Heb 4:14-16)

Have you ever felt so guilty that you didn't think you could actually talk to God about it? "He's not going to want to listen to me repent for that *again*." "God could never forgive me for *that*." Well, it depends. Is the God you don't think wants to talk to you the one who sent his Son Jesus Christ? If so, then listen carefully: self-hatred is not holiness. I believe a lie from the devil himself when I think that God is most glorified when I am most guilty and miserable before him. And most importantly for Hebrews, when I believe that lie, I deny that Jesus actually stands in heaven to intercede on my behalf and welcome me into the presence of his Father.

I *can* approach God in prayer, even if it means confessing the same thing for the hundredth time, because my priest is there to mediate forgiveness and encourage me to follow his example and conquer temptation the next time. And I *must* do so for the same reason—temptation will keep coming, and only by following the example of the faithful one who stands with his Father can I overcome it. Notice, again, that Jesus is *with* his Father. There's no option for asking Jesus to do the approaching for me so I can stay at a safe distance (call it the Mosaic option). You can't have the Son and avoid the Father.

"But what if I've done something *really* bad?" Go back to Hebrews 12:18-21. If you took the time to check all of the descriptions of Mount

Sinai against their Old Testament sources, you'd find that all of them come from Exodus 19 or Deuteronomy 4–5 (which describe what Israel experienced when God descended on Mount Sinai and spoke the Ten Commandments). All of them, that is, except the description of Moses: "I am trembling with fear" (Heb 12:21). If you have cross-references in your Bible, it probably tells you to go to Deuteronomy 9:19 for this one— and if you go there, you'll discover that Moses didn't say this when God initially came down on the mountain but when he was mediating for Israel after they committed idolatry by worshiping the golden calf a few weeks after that initial encounter.[3] Why is this important? In the face of one of Israel's greatest sins, their mediator stands tremblingly in the presence of God and begs for mercy—and God granted his request. If God on Moses' account forgives Israel for such mind-boggling stupidity, if I can put it that way, how much more will he listen to your mediator, his own Son, no matter how catastrophic your failure has been? Go to your God in prayer and trust the promise of your mediator that his blood speaks forgiveness and grace rather than condemnation.

God's Presence and the Supper

A second way we enter God's presence, according to Hebrews, is Communion (a.k.a. the Lord's Supper, the Eucharist, etc.). What the Bible says about Communion, and how the church has interpreted it over the centuries, is complicated. Actually, if you're familiar at all with those debates, you know *complicated* is an understatement. Transubstantiation, consubstantiation, real presence, ubiquity of Christ—I have no intention of settling those debates here. My hope in these few paragraphs is simply to give you a vision for what Communion might look like if we let Hebrews—as it relates to Deuteronomy—have a voice in the conversation.

Go back to Deuteronomy. The covenant has been established in blood (Ex 24:8) and celebrated with a meal (Ex 24:11), but it needs to

---

[3]Michael H. Kibbe, *Godly Fear or Ungodly Failure? Hebrews 12 and the Sinai Theophanies*, Beihefte zur Zeitschrift für die neutestamentliche Wissenschaft 216 (Berlin: de Gruyter, 2016), 200-201.

be reenacted so the people of God can be renewed in their commitment to it. That reenactment took place when Israel stood on the plains of Moab, heard Moses speak, and committed themselves to the covenant established at Sinai. In that moment, they were experiencing Sinai all over again. And when they came together every seven years to read "this law" to every single person in the land, they experienced it all over again (Deut 31:9-13). And again. And again. This isn't legalistic ritual. This is a tremendous gift: a way to celebrate and relive the moment when God purified them with blood and entered into relationship with them. "You have now become the people of Yahweh your God!" (Deut 27:9).

Now look to Hebrews. The covenant was established on a mountain (Mount Zion), and the blood presented there purifies us and makes us fit for relationship with God. Hebrews 12:22 says we "have come" to that mountain. Not "will come," or "might hopefully someday come." *Have* come. In the context not only of the original exhortation but every time we read Hebrews aloud as God's people (like the Israelites rereading Deuteronomy every so often), *we are at the mountain, watching the covenant-making ceremony unfold once more.* Sounds a bit familiar, doesn't it? "This cup is the new covenant in my blood. . . . Whenever you drink it, do so in remembrance of me" (1 Cor 11:25).

It shouldn't surprise us that many have wondered whether Hebrews was a sermon specifically written to accompany the Lord's Supper.[4] We don't have enough concrete evidence to say that with certainty. But we can say, I think, once we've put Hebrews alongside 1 Corinthians and the Gospel stories of the Last Supper, that to partake of the Supper is to reenact the covenant. No new blood is spilled, as though Christ needed to be offered repeatedly (both the parallel with Deuteronomy and the explicit prohibitions against it in Heb 6:6; 10:25-26 make this extremely clear)—again, that's the difference between a reenactment and a do-over. And yet in that moment we are transported to the

---

[4]John J. Davis, *Worship and the Reality of God: An Evangelical Theology of Real Presence* (Downers Grove, IL: InterVarsity Press, 2010), 174-75.

Upper Room, to the foot of the cross, to the heavenly sanctuary itself, watching the Son offer himself to the Father to atone for our sins and prepare a place for us.

Back to the main point: according to Hebrews, in taking the elements of Communion we find ourselves in the presence of God. He is present with us, or, rather, we are present with him. You can't reenact the covenant without the covenant mediator. And remember what Paul says in 1 Corinthians 11:27-30 about abusing the body of Christ (= the church) while participating in the body of Christ (= the bread and cup)? When you proclaim the covenant with your lips and break the covenant with your actions, you do precisely what Israel did when it read Deuteronomy and sang the song while committing idolatry and injustice: you eat and drink judgment on yourself (1 Cor 11:29).

It's crucial for us to notice that Israel's sin, like that of the Corinthian church, wasn't always vertical—by which I mean directed toward God himself. Idolatry is a huge problem in the Old Testament, but it wasn't the only problem. Sometimes Israel worshiped the one true God, which was great, but in the same moment committed terrible acts of injustice, and God rejected their worship and punished them as covenant breakers. That's the concern in Corinth as well: they weren't committing idolatry, technically speaking, when they took the bread and the cup, but they were committing injustice toward some in their community and in doing so violating the covenant as surely as if they were offering their praises to another god altogether.

When we enter God's presence in Communion, to reenact the covenant and recommit to it, we need to keep in mind that our covenant faithfulness is as much a function of our relationships with our brother or sister as it is of our direct relationship with God. "Whoever claims to love God but hates their brother or sister," says the apostle John, "is a liar" (1 Jn 4:20). Little wonder, then, that Jesus says, "If you bring your gift to the altar, but there remember that your brother or sister has something against you, leave your gift at the altar and go first to be reconciled with your brother or sister—*then*, go and offer your gift" (Mt 5:23-24).

The really scary part, though, is that avoiding God's presence out of guilt ("I've not been particularly kind to my wife this week, so I'd better just not take Communion") isn't one of the choices. Deuteronomy never says, "And if you feel like you haven't quite measured up recently, just stand silently while those around you sing the song." Nope. Not an option. No giving up on gathering together as God's people to celebrate your covenant with him (Heb 10:25). We *will* come into God's presence, and we *will* be held accountable for our faithfulness to the covenant—both as it concerns our vertical relationship with God himself and as it concerns our horizontal relationships with our brothers and sisters. And I must say, that quick moment of confession many of us have been taught to do right before Communion so we don't "eat and drink unworthily" is missing the point. I don't mean God doesn't forgive confessed sin—I mean that's not at all what Paul is talking about when he talks about the kind of covenant reenactment that merits God's judgment. He isn't saying, "If you sinned this morning and haven't yet confessed it, you're about to spit in the face of the covenant." He is saying, "Your covenant faithfulness is as much a function of your right treatment of God's people around you as it is of directing your worship toward the right God, so when you reenact the covenant and hate your brother and sister, you are pronouncing your own death sentence." To be present with God in the taking of bread and wine requires that we see ourselves as present not only with God but with many others whom Jesus calls brothers and sisters along with us.

God's Presence in Eternity

Israel kept reenacting the covenant in the land because the land wasn't the final destination—because the mutual giving of life from land to people and people to land remained unrealized. And the same is true for us, even as we gather and formally reenact the covenant and receive life from God through the body and blood of Jesus given once for all. Meaning: that reenactment is a signpost backward, to the inauguration of the covenant, but it's also a signpost forward, to its consummation.

We will not always be ectopic. Hebrews has a third and final way of referring to God's presence. Hebrews 11–12 describes our journey after

Jesus as an endurance race, a walk by faith of indeterminate length. But someday our endurance race will come to an end, and we'll finally enter God's rest (Heb 4:6-11). Someday the unshaken kingdom will be ours (Heb 12:25-28), the enemies of Jesus will finally be subdued under his feet (Heb 1:13), and "all manner of thing shall be well."[5] And when that happens, we'll be in his presence in a new and unimaginably glorious way.

In recent years we've begun to hear more and more about an alternate vision for eternity than the "disembodied souls in heaven singing hymns forever" sort of eschatology many of us got from Sunday school (whether or not that's what our Sunday school teachers actually said). We're being reminded, thankfully, that God does not snatch us away from material existence to live forever, disembodied, in heaven.[6] Rather, what he designed humanity to do in the first place (govern his creation as his representatives) is precisely what he plans for us to do once the story of redemption reaches its final chapter. We will be bodily resurrected so that we can take up our mission of being stewards and image bearers in God's redeemed material world. Hebrews clearly points in this direction: the task of saved humanity is to govern the world that is to come—to receive the "glory and honor" of stewarding the new creation (Heb 2:8-10).

As healthy a corrective as this is, we must not forget that behind the sometimes absurd images of an immaterial heavenly choir is a significant biblical truth: we have indeed been called into communion with the Creator, and to gaze on his face forever is indeed the highest good imaginable for a creature.[7] As Paul puts it, "Right now we see dimly, like we're looking at a reflection in a [not-particularly-well-polished] mirror; then we will see face to face. Right now my knowledge is incomplete, but then I will know fully like I am fully known" (1 Cor 13:12). Endless contemplation of God might not sound like much of an upgrade from an

---

[5]Julian of Norwich, *Revelations of Divine Love* (London: Methuen, 1901), 56.

[6]Perhaps the most influential spokesperson for this point is N. T. Wright, particularly in his book *Surprised by Hope: Rethinking Heaven, the Resurrection, and the Mission of the Church* (New York: HarperOne), 2008.

[7]On this "beatific vision," as it has traditionally been called, see Michael Allen, *Grounded in Heaven: Recentering Christian Hope and Life on God* (Grand Rapids, MI: Eerdmans, 2018).

endless hymn sing (minus the out-of-tune piano) until you consider exactly what's being proposed: uninhibited and ever-increasing intimacy with our Father.

It's a both/and. We will live in the material world as embodied creatures who rule over the works of God's hands. And we will receive life through that location rather than in spite of it, because we will be in unhindered communion with our Creator. He will be with us, and we will be with him, and there will be no more need of any signposts, because we will have arrived.

Study Questions

1. When you use the phrase "the presence of God," or think about being "with God," what do you usually mean by that?

2. Have you ever struggled to pray because you didn't think God would want to have the same conversation *again* about your sin? Have you ever avoided God out of guilt?

3. How does thinking about communion as a reenactment change the way you might participate in it?

4. When you imagine eternity, does it include unhindered connection with God himself in addition to being restored as stewards of his creation?

13

FEELING OUT OF PLACE?

I HAD A CONVERSATION WITH GOD recently that went something like this:

Me: I don't want to be a slave to fear.

God: Are you fearful in your parenting?

Me: I'm reactionary. Is that the same thing?

God: Yes. Because your reactions are insecurity, frustration, passivity, laziness, and fear. What are you afraid of?

Me: That they'll fail to follow you.

God: Stop trying to determine the final outcome. Do the right thing moment by moment. That's what ectopic people whom I am keeping alive do.

Me: I don't trust myself to do that.

God: Then what you fear is your failures, not your kids' failures.

Me: Yeah.

God: Then what you really fear is that I won't do what I promised. Because I promised to overcome your failures.

I promised to overcome your failures. That's not a bad summary of Hebrews in relation to Deuteronomy. Deuteronomy is about Israel's failures and God's inevitable response to those failures. We tend to think that what's changed from then to now is God's character—he used to be just, now he's merciful; he used to be mean, now he's nice; whatever.

Complete and total nonsense, as far as Hebrews is concerned. That's not what's changed. Same God.

So, what's changed? Well, the consequences for failure have changed, but not in the direction you might have expected: they're worse. Every time Hebrews warns us about the consequences of disobedience, it uses phrases from Deuteronomy such as "vengeance is mine" and "God is a consuming fire" and "dies without mercy." So let us have no more of the absurd idea that God has gone soft. If anything, on a practical level, it's the other way around: *How much worse* punishment does the new covenant breaker deserve than the old covenant breaker (Heb 10:29)? Remember Deuteronomy 28? Worse than that. And that was pretty bad.

God gave Israel a mediator, Moses, and a whole succession of prophets like Moses (Deut 18:15-18), who would continually bring them back to the covenant. But when they rejected those mediators, God then provided a new covenant, with a better mediator—Jesus. So if you rejected the old covenant, another grace still remained: the new covenant. But what about us? If we reject the new covenant and its mediator, what then? There will never be a *new* new covenant. There will never be another mediator other than the one we now have. Say no to Moses? God gives Jesus. Say no to Jesus? "There no longer remains any sacrifice for sins, but rather a terrifying expectation of judgment and a zealous fire that will consume God's enemies" (Heb 10:26-27).

We really ought to pause right there. It's good for us to fear God. It's right for us to quake a little bit when we think about getting *that* close to him. It forces us to ask some hard questions about our fitness for his presence. But the real question isn't, Am I fit for God's presence? The real question is, How is it that I *am* fit for his presence? Because I am in fact able to draw near. If I weren't, he would have told me to stay away, like he did to Israel at Sinai: "Go down, Moses, and warn the people that they must not cross the barrier to see Yahweh, and perish in doing so" (Ex 19:21). The first command has always been, "Let not what is unholy come close to the holy God." But now the second command is, "You, come close to the holy God." Unless God is playing tricks and trying to get us to come close so he can zap us, it must be that those who are called to approach are in fact fit to do so. But again—what's changed? Three things have changed. The first is that there's been a serious mediatorial upgrade. No offense to Moses, because he did some amazing things for Israel at Mount Sinai. But he's not the Creator of the universe, the heir of the world to come, the high priest who cleansed the heavenly sanctuary with his own blood, the Son of God, the same yesterday and today and forever, everything that Hebrews says about Jesus.

Moses did pretty well considering what he had to work with, but at the end of the day, even he knew he wouldn't get the job done—and said so himself when he told Israel that they'd ditch the covenant and bring down God's anger before the dust settled over his corpse (Deut 31:27). That's part of the problem, isn't it? Moses' corpse. Our mediator doesn't have one of those. He didn't appoint any successors, any backups, anyone to try to fill his shoes after he was gone because the work would outlast him. He'll never die, never retire, never walk away from the mission. The other difference is a qualitative one: Moses was a faithful *servant*, but Jesus was a faithful *Son* (Heb 3:5-6). Think about it: Could God call Jesus his Son (Heb 1:5) in one breath and in the next reject those the Son calls his siblings (Heb 2:11)?

That's the first difference between our situation and Israel's: a better mediator. Here's the second: a better heart. Watch the pattern:

Who will give them a heart like this to fear me and to keep all my commands forever? (Deut 5:29)

Even to this day, *Yahweh has not given you a heart* to know or eyes to see or ears to hear. (Deut 29:4)

Now jump ahead in the story to Jeremiah and Ezekiel, as God promises postexilic restoration to his people.

I will give to them a heart to know me—that I am Yahweh. (Jer 24:7)

I will put the fear of me in their hearts, so that they will never turn away from me. (Jer 32:40)

I will give you a new heart, and I will put a new spirit in you; I will remove the heart of stone from you and give you a fleshy heart. (Ezek 36:26).

And, of course, Hebrews, twice quoting Jeremiah 31:

This is the covenant that I will make with the house of Israel

after those days, says the Lord:

"*I will put my laws on their minds*

and write them on their hearts." (Heb 8:10; 10:16, quoting Jer 31:33)

What *didn't* happen at Sinai, what Jeremiah and Ezekiel prophesied *would* happen and Hebrews claims *did* happen in the new covenant, is that God's Spirit has transformed stony, rebellious hearts into soft, obedient hearts, so that we are now able to fear God and be receptive to his commands.[1]

The third and final change from Deuteronomy to Hebrews follows logically from the other two. If Jesus will do some things that Moses couldn't, and I can do some things that Israel couldn't, the endless pessimism of Deuteronomy just doesn't fit in Hebrews.

From the day you left Egypt until you arrived at this very place [the plains of Moab], you have been rebellious against Yahweh. (Deut 9:7)

You have been rebellious against Yahweh as long as I have known you. (Deut 9:24)

[Israel] will forsake me and break my covenant that I have made with them. (Deut 31:16)

I know their evil intentions even before I bring them into the land that I have promised to give them. (Deut 31:21)

I [Moses] know how rebellious and stubborn you are! If you've been this rebellious while I am alive with you, how much more so after I die! . . . I know that after I die you will certainly become

---

[1]Paul's apostolic defense in 2 Cor 3:1–4:6 is essentially a commentary on precisely this heart-transforming work of the Spirit.

corrupt and turn from the way I have commanded you to go.
(Deut 31:27-29)

And on and on it goes—there is no doubt whatsoever in God's mind, or
in Moses' mind, that Israel will not wait long before it forsakes God and
their covenant with him, inevitably bringing all the disasters and curses
down on their heads. It's *guaranteed* to happen. But what about Hebrews? Look at Hebrews 6:7-8, which doesn't quote Deuteronomy but
uses Deuteronomic language (Deut 11:26-28; 29:23-24) to describe the
consequences of disobedience: "For the ground that drinks of the rain
that often falls on it and produces a crop that is useful to those for whom
it is cultivated—that ground receives a blessing from God. But if the
ground produces thorns and thistles, it is worthless and in danger of
being cursed, and in the end it will be burned." Typical of the warning
passages, right? God's judgment falls on you, and you deserved it. But
look at the next verse: "But we are convinced, brothers and sisters, even
though we speak like this, that better things will come from you—things
that accompany salvation" (Heb 6:9). This is about the most un-Deuter-
onomic thing the author of Hebrews could possibly have said.[2] Deuteronomy follows its warnings with, "And we all know you're going to fail
and all these curses are going to come on you." But Hebrews follows its
warnings with, "And I'm confident none of this is going to happen to
you." Not because I don't ever fail. I do, and I will. But because he
promises to overcome my failures.

This is the promise we receive from Hebrews: not that our struggle
with sin is over but that in the struggle we will emerge as conquerors
rather than the conquered. What is required of us is that we do indeed
struggle, all the while keeping our eyes on our mediator, who has ascended to his Father (and our Father!) and who calls us to stay faithful
so that we can follow him there. "Choose life." *Choose* life. Life apparently
isn't just an automatic thing once the covenant has been inaugurated.

---

[2]Michael H. Kibbe, *Godly Fear or Ungodly Failure? Hebrews 12 and the Sinai Theophanies*,
Beihefte zur Zeitschrift für die neutestamentliche Wissenschaft 216 (Berlin: de Gruyter,
2016), 135.

Hebrews is quite concerned that we would refuse God's life, that we would think, absurd as it sounds, that we could somehow supply our own life in the midst of our ectopicness. Can a man dying of thirst conjure up water in the desert? Foolish, to be sure, but no less common on account of its foolishness. Every other source of life is a mirage, but mirages can be pretty convincing.

He promises to overcome our failures. He promised to keep us alive. He knows we're living in a lifeless world—that's not news to him. He knows we're out of place, and he knows that the place in which we are is trying to kill us. He knows that, left to ourselves, we die. So he didn't leave us to ourselves. He gave us his Son. He gave us his Spirit. He gave us new hearts. He gave us covenant reenactment ceremonies. He gave us communities of faith to encourage us and challenge us and speak his Word to us. These are the mechanisms by which God will keep his promise to keep us alive and, eventually, bring us into the fullness of life.

Study Questions

1. God will overcome your failures. Is this hard for you to believe? Why?

2. Meditate on God's Word to you, coming as it does from the context of the difference between Deuteronomy and Hebrews: "*But we are convinced, brothers and sisters, even though we speak like this, that better things will come from you—things that accompany salvation*" (Heb 6:9).

SECTION 4

PUTTING (JESUS')
LIFE ON DISPLAY

MY SONS LOVE SPORTS. They're in that stage of life where the toughest decision they feel the need to make is whether to be professional baseball players or professional basketball players. They're both reasonably good athletes, for an eight-year-old and a thirteen-year-old. But you and I know that this particular decision is going to take care of itself, right? As their dad, I don't feel the need to rain on this parade just yet. Chances are good that reality will set in just fine, like it has for so many millions of other young athletes.

As a former wannabe collegiate athlete, I used to shake my head at people who could have made the team but decided not to. I couldn't fathom saying no to an athletic scholarship or a spot on the roster simply because I cared more about doing something else. Once I was in the basketball offices at my university (I'd achieved "practice dummy and equipment manager" status) and the head coach commented to the assistant coach, "Can you imagine how hard Mike would have worked if we'd given him a spot on the roster?" And I stood there thinking, "If you knew that about me, why didn't you?!"

Thank God for unanswered prayers, right? I adored basketball. I idolized basketball. It was my lifeline, my dream. And that dream needed to die, because either it was going to die or I was. Grace sometimes comes in the form of cutting off the supply of a false lifeline. Grace is the prodigal son running out of money just before a famine hits. Grace is me *not* making the Cedarville University varsity men's basketball team. Grace is

God taking away from us whatever we've been using to stay alive that wasn't going to fulfill that calling anyway.[1]

Having said that, God doesn't tend to simply remove temptation; in fact, he more frequently invites us to endure it. He never leaves us to die in the wilderness, but he does invite us to journey through the wilderness, to be tempted by its mirages, to hold on to the truth and reject the lies. It isn't always fun, and it isn't often easy. "This calls for endurance and faithfulness on the part of God's people" (Rev 13:10). Or, to put it in Hebrews' own terms, "Let us run with perseverance the race marked out for us" (Heb 12:1).

Hebrews really requires two kinds of perseverance. One kind is simply to wade through the sermon itself, in addition to tracking with whoever your guide on that journey might be. Thanks for sticking with me so far! Hebrews can be difficult—difficult to understand, difficult to accept, and difficult to know how to put into practice. Fortunately, some of the later portions of Hebrews are here to remedy that last problem, but in doing so they're also going to confront us with the need to persevere in another way: the way of obedience. Surviving ectopic life isn't an abstraction. "Fix your eyes on Jesus" (Heb 12:2) isn't a meaningless platitude or vague idea that's supposed to make us feel better. It's something we're supposed to *do*, in very specific and concrete terms. And if you're starving for those terms, get ready for a feast.

---

[1] I don't mean that hopes and dreams just *are* pursuits of life where it may not be found. I mean that we are extremely capable of turning them into that, as I did with basketball.

14

FAITH IN A LIFELESS WORLD

IT'S A CLASSIC CINEMATIC MOMENT. *Indiana Jones and the Last Crusade.* Harrison Ford, a.k.a. Dr. Indiana Jones, comes out of a tunnel and nearly topples headlong into an endless chasm. A hundred feet wide, a million miles deep. On the other side of that one hundred feet is the continuation of the tunnel—but there's no bridge. How to get from A to B? "Only with a leap from the lion's head will he prove his worth . . . the leap of faith." So Jones stands at the edge, closes his eyes, extends his left foot out over the chasm, and leans forward. And, of course, he finds himself standing firmly on a nearly invisible bridge that spans the gap and permits him to move forward in his quest for the holy grail.

The leap of faith. How often do we use that phrase? Step out into the unknown, trust God, take a leap of faith—and you'll land on the invisible bridge. It's a powerful image. But it isn't a realistic one. Ever taken a leap of faith? Ever taken a risk, hoping and trusting that the path that you sensed God leading you down was the right one? Sure you have. Ah, but here's the question: once you leaped, how long did it take for you to land? In the movie, it's nearly instantaneous. From the moment that Indiana Jones leans forward and commits to the unknown, it's less than a second before he discovers, to his delight, that he will not be plummeting to his death. In the movie, the time between the *leap* and the *land* is almost no time at all. In real life? Could be minutes. Could be months. Could be decades.

There are really two problems here. The first is that between the leap and the land comes an unknown amount of time. I once left my home in Dallas to "see about a girl," as another classic cinematic moment puts it. I first visited northern California in November 2004. Her father walked her down the aisle in May 2007. From leap to land—two and a half years. Worth every minute, in hindsight; but it's not like I put in my notice at work in Texas in the morning and got married in California that afternoon. It's quite rare, in fact, for leaps of faith to land quickly.

The second problem is that there isn't always a definitive land at all. I'll share more of the story as this part unfolds, but a few years ago I helped start a new university. That was a leap of faith, to be sure—but when does it land? How many years does Great Northern University need to remain in business for the leap to have been worth it? How many students does it need to educate? How big does the endowment need to get? To put it in biblical terms: At what point does the faith of starting this school become sight? There have been many celebratory moments in the Great Northern University journey, but they're mile markers, not finish lines. They are reminders of the continued need for faith, not in-dications that the need for faith has been eliminated.

This is the real problem with leap-land thinking: that there's a clear moment when faith becomes sight, when we can sit back and say, "Yes, our faith was confirmed because God came through for us, and it was all worth it," *and that moment happens in this life*. It doesn't. Glimpses of eternity do happen. Momentary confirmations do happen. But if we envision life as mostly straightforward with the occasional need to step out in faith for a second, we're missing how ectopic life really works.

The question is not how to skip ahead to the end, when we're no longer ectopic. The question is how to *endure*. And the answer to that question is indeed faith. Not the leap of faith but the walk of faith. The wait of faith. Faith for the long haul. Faith for the inevitable stumbles and struggles. Not faith for getting out of here as quickly as possible but faith to persevere for as long as God would sustain us in our current state. How do we attain to such faith? Hebrews would love to tell us.

Divine Oaths

God spoke. That's the whole book of Hebrews in a nutshell. And you might also remember that there's an interesting distinction in Hebrews between God speaking and God speaking *with an oath* (Heb 7:20-21, 28). That sometimes God spoke with an oath, and sometimes he didn't, doesn't mean the times where he didn't are less reliable or less trustworthy, or anything like that. It just means he wanted to make it *really, abundantly, excessively* obvious to us that he meant what he said.

In Hebrews 7 God swore an oath to his Son: "The Lord has sworn, and will not change his mind: you are a priest forever [like Melchizedek]'" (Heb 7:21, quoting Ps 110:4). The point, in that context, is that there is absolutely no possibility whatsoever that God will turn a deaf ear to the intercession his Son offers for us. God will not give up on us, because he will not give up on Jesus.

Psalm 110:4, quoted in reference to Jesus' appointment as high priest, isn't the only divine oath in Hebrews. There are two others. The first is in Hebrews 3:11 (and the same again in Heb 3:18; 4:3), where God says (quoting Ps 95:11), "I swore in my wrath: they will never enter my rest." There was a group of people whom God brought out of slavery who didn't believe he could finish the job and bring them into the Promised Land. We've already spent some time in Deuteronomy, so think back to that story. Psalm 95 is about the parents of those who participated in the covenant reenactment ceremony in Deuteronomy—it's the generation that came out of Egypt and went to Mount Sinai but *didn't* enter the land.

That generation grumbled, complained, begged, blasphemed, you name it. It's a train wreck of a community, from start to finish. So many problems. But Hebrews summarizes all of those sins and shortcomings like this: "They were not able to enter [the Promised Land] because of unbelief" (Heb 3:19). Unbelief. Lack of faith. Hold that thought.

The other divine oath in Hebrews happens in Hebrews 6:13-14, this time quoting Genesis 22:17: "I will surely bless you and multiply you." Wait, you might say—there's nothing in this quote about swearing an oath. But if we look back just one verse, to Genesis 22:16, we find God saying this:

"By myself I have sworn, says the Lord, because you have done this thing and not withheld your beloved son from me, I will surely bless you."

You know the story. God asked Abraham to give Isaac to him as a sacrifice. Abraham obeyed, believing that God somehow knew what he was doing, but just before he killed Isaac, an angel stopped him and provided a ram for the sacrifice in place of Isaac. Oh, the questions that ought to arise when we consider that series of events![1] For now, though, the main thing is the oath: "Because God wanted to make the unchanging nature of his purpose very clear to the heirs of what was promised, he confirmed it with an oath" (Heb 6:17).

Three oaths. One to Abraham (Gen 22:17), one to Israel (Ps 95:11), one to Jesus (Ps 110:4). Two prompted by faithfulness (Abraham and Jesus), one prompted by lack thereof (Israel).

Maybe we could think of it this way. God swore an oath to Abraham about his descendants. The question is not whether God will keep his promise to those descendants. He will. The question is who those descendants will be. That question is a question about faith, faith like Abraham had faith. Like the apostle Paul said, "The promise comes by faith, so that it may be by grace and may be guaranteed to all Abraham's offspring—not only to those who are of the law but also to those who have the faith of Abraham. He is the father of us all" (Rom 4:16 NIV). In other words, we have a two-part relationship to Abraham: that he received a promise of offspring, and those offspring are precisely those who imitate his faith.

Back to Hebrews and the oaths. On the one hand: if we have faith like Abraham, we look from God's promise to Abraham ahead to God's promise to Jesus, because the high-priestly oath to Jesus is the *how* to the *what* of the Abrahamic oath. *How* will God guarantee blessing to Abraham's offspring? Through Jesus, seated at God's right hand. When

---

[1] If you want some technical, brilliant, and provocative explorations of those questions, see J. Richard Middleton, *Abraham's Silence: The Binding of Isaac, the Suffering of Job, and How to Talk Back to God* (Grand Rapids, MI: Baker Academic, 2021); Jon D. Levenson, *The Death and Resurrection of the Beloved Son: The Transformation of Child Sacrifice in Judaism and Christianity* (New Haven, CT: Yale University Press, 1993).

these two oaths are linked by faith, we see that God absolutely cannot, will not, fail to do what he has said he will do.

On the other hand: if we do not have faith like Abraham, we look from God's promise to Abraham ahead to God's promise to the exodus/ wilderness generation, because that is the fate of those who have been invited to be Abraham's descendants but who have not imitated his faith. When *these* two oaths are linked, we see that God absolutely cannot, will not, fail to judge those who reject his ability to do what he has said he will do.

He's talking about the final assizes: when the chaos and complexity of life under the sun is brought to an end, when truly, fully, "The kingdoms of this world will have become the kingdom of our Lord and of his Messiah" (Rev 11:15), as John put it. We live once, we die once, "and then the judgment" (Heb 9:27). And in the judgment, there will only be two options: either I have belief like Abraham, or I have unbelief like the Israelites in the wilderness. The word of God echoing in my ear in that moment will either be, "You will never enter my rest!" or, "He is your priest forever!"

Faith Beyond Life, Faith Beyond Death

"Faith is made valuable by its object." I don't know how many times I heard Dr. Richard Blumenstock say this, way back in my undergraduate days at Cedarville University. "Faith is made valuable by its object." *There can be miracles if you believe* (speaking of Hollywood intrusions into biblical themes)—ridiculous. There can be miracles if you rightly believe in someone who can and does perform miracles. "Faith is made valuable by its object," meaning it's a good idea to believe, to have faith in something or someone, if what you believe about that something or someone is *true*. My faith in God is entirely useless if I don't believe anything in particular about him, and worse than useless if what I believe about him is incorrect.

So that's the crucial question: What must I believe about God? I can't just have faith "in God." I must have faith "in God who ____." We could put quite a lot of things in that blank space. We could jump over to Paul's letters and find all sorts of right and useful answers to the question, What must I believe about God? But Paul and the author of Hebrews agree, especially when the faith in question is the sort of faith that puts us in the lineage of Abraham, that we must above all things believe in the God who raises the dead.

Paul identifies us as "those who have the faith of Abraham" (Rom 4:16). It goes on to say that Abraham "is our father in the sight of God, in whom he believed—the God who gives life to the dead" (Rom 4:17 NIV). And then, a little later, Abraham "faced the fact that his body was as good as dead. . . . Yet he did not waver through unbelief regarding the promise of God, but was strengthened in his faith and gave glory to God, being fully persuaded that God had power to do what he had promised" (Rom 4:19-21 NIV). Abraham and Sarah were dead as far as the ability to produce new biological life from their bodies. God had promised that he was going to produce new biological life from their bodies. They believed that he was able to make life emerge out of death. And God did precisely that, vindicating their faith.

Hebrews 11. We'll start with Abraham, but what we see with him is going to turn out to be the key to the whole chapter. "By faith Abraham offered up Isaac when he was tested. He, who had received the promise, offered his only son—the one about whom God said, 'In Isaac your offspring will be named.' He did this because he figured that God was able to raise the dead, and, in a sense, he did receive Isaac back from death" (Heb 11:17-19). Same thing as Romans 4. Abraham's faith is specifically in the God who can raise the dead, and God will do precisely that if that's what it takes to keep his promises. But why? Why is believing that God raises the dead so important?

Let's go back to Hebrews 1–2 for a moment. Jesus stepped down into our ectopic state. He temporarily relinquished his grip on human life— he voluntarily cut himself off from the lifeline that was rightfully his from the beginning, you might say, so as to experience the inevitable outcome of life in a lifeless world: death. But by his own divine power he brought humanity out of death and back into life, thereby making ectopic life something other than a contradiction in terms. He ascended to his Father and now sits at his Father's right hand as the perpetual source of life with God that we all desperately need in our misplaced state. This is why Hebrews will say, "By the grace of God, Jesus tasted death for everyone" (Heb 2:9), and "By his death, Jesus broke the power of him who holds the power of death" and thereby "frees those who all their lives were held in slavery by their fear of death" (Heb 2:14-15).

You and I were created by God to live with God and to be givers of his life just as we been recipients of it. But that's not happening. All is not well with the world. We as humans are not pouring out God's life into the world around us precisely because we are not properly positioned to receive it. We are ectopic, and therefore we are dying. And because we are dying, and because we know we are dying, we grasp at anything that might appear to us to be a lifeline. But all this is spitting into the wind. Like an unborn baby whose desperate struggle for life serves only to accelerate his mother's demise, our search for life where it may not be found only deepens the woundedness of the world around us.

We look for meaning in romantic partnerships but destroy both partners. We look for fulfillment in our professions, but instead we are consumed by performance pressures and the outcome turns out not to be that great anyway. We think that happiness will come with raising children, but what we get instead is codependencies and prodigal sons and empty-nester divorces—not to mention that raising kids is unbelievably hard under the best of circumstances. Every supposedly life-giving pursuit can be a mirage. In the end, it all leads to death. It's all meaningless, vanity, emptiness, whatever word your Bible uses at the beginning of Ecclesiastes, because we're asking something to be an ultimate source of life that could never have served that purpose.

And so, we are destined to death—unless something outside us, outside our world, keeps us alive in it. This is what Jesus accomplished when he lived like we do, died like we will, but then rose and ascended so that our life would be "hidden with Christ in God," as Paul says

(Col 3:3). If God were not the sort of God who could be trusted to raise the dead, none of this works very well. Christ would still be dead (problem one). We would surely expect to stay dead once we got there (problem two). And there would be nothing to stimulate any particular way of living in the present, given that nothing we do now would make any difference to our inevitable demise in the near future (problem three). This is why it matters so much that we have the faith of Abraham: faith that God can and does and will bring life into death.

But what does it mean, exactly, to "have the faith of Abraham"? Even though our word *faith* and our word *belief* both come from the same Greek word in the New Testament, we should not therefore assume that faith simply means "believing that something is true." I believe all sorts of things, with varying degrees of confidence, that have no bearing on how I conduct myself. I believe Pluto is a ball of ice and rock that orbits the sun just past Neptune. I believe the Boston Celtics are going to win the NBA championship in the near future.[2] I do believe these things, and I have no intention whatsoever of acting on those beliefs, other than to state them, as I just have. But faith, in Hebrews, means a whole lot more than that. So let's go to the most famous part of Hebrews, Hebrews 11, the "hall of faith," and see what it says about how to live, ectopically, by faith.

The first thing worth noticing is something my friend Bryan Dyer pointed out to me a couple of years ago: Hebrews 11 is absolutely stuffed with references to death.[3]

By faith Abel spoke even after he died (Heb 11:4).

By faith Enoch didn't die (Heb 11:5).

By faith Noah saved his family from death (Heb 11:7).

By faith Abraham had kids even when procreatively dead (Heb 11:12).

---

[2]Update: it happened.

[3]Bryan Dyer has also put this point in print in his excellent essay "'All of These Died in Faith': Hebrews 11 and Faith in the Face of Death," *Catholic Biblical Quarterly* 83 (2021): 638-54.

People lived by faith even up to the point at which they died (Heb 11:13).

By faith Abraham received Isaac back from death (Heb 11:19).

By faith Isaac blessed his sons regarding their future after he was dead (Heb 11:20).

By faith Jacob blessed Joseph's sons when he was dying (Heb 11:21).

By faith Joseph spoke about the exodus that would happen after he died (Heb 11:22).

By faith Moses' parents saved him from death (Heb 11:23).

By faith Israel was saved from death through the Passover (Heb 11:28).

By faith Israel survived the Red Sea, but the Egyptians died (Heb 11:29).

By faith Rahab alone escaped death in Jericho (Heb 11:31).

By faith various prophets escaped various forms of death (Heb 11:32-33).

By faith some women received back their dead (Heb 11:35).

By faith other women died in hope of a later resurrection (Heb 11:35).

Various prophets maintained faith even as they died in horrific ways (Heb 11:36-37).

That's a *lot* of references to death. I don't think it's an overstatement to say that faith, in Hebrews 11, simply is the proper human response to the threat of death. But what is the outcome of that response? What's the payoff to having faith? It depends.

Sometimes having faith means you don't have to die (Enoch).

Sometimes having faith means you don't have to die *yet* (Isaac).

Sometimes having faith means having insight into what happens after you die (Joseph).

Sometimes having faith means knowing that death isn't the last word (lots of people).

Four different tracks. Two include not dying right now, two include dying right now. Clearly faith isn't a cheat code to an easy life. Odds are, we will die (Enoch being the exception that proves the rule). Faith isn't a denial of cold, hard reality, like thinking that if I believe hard enough, I can jump off a ten-story building and land unharmed. Faith, because it is faith in the God who raises the dead, is a way of looking at death.

Everyone in Hebrews 11 assumes that death is defeatable. If God wants to take Enoch straight to heaven, he can do that, and there's nothing Death can do to stop him. If God wants to hold back the waters of chaos and permit his people to walk across the sea floor unharmed, he can do that, and there's nothing Death can do to stop him.

The inhabitants of the hall of faith share a second assumption: not just that death *can be* defeated but that it *will be* defeated. In the short term it is defeated by progeny: the line of Abraham lives on in his descendants. And in the long term it is defeated by what Hebrews 11:35 calls the "better resurrection." Lazarus walked out of the grave when Jesus called him, but at some point in the years that followed, he was carried back in. But a day is coming in which we who are of the faith of Abraham will rise not like Lazarus but like Jesus: to indestructible life (Heb 7:16). Death has become a holding pattern, a liminal state—not a residence unto itself but a temporary location out of which we will one day walk when Jesus calls our names.

So—what is faith? Faith is having a proper perspective on death. Faith is not denying death, because death is real and terrible and generally inevitable. But faith is also not submitting to death, because death is a defeated enemy. We can't stay dead, because one who has already died and risen is keeping us alive. Faith is staring death in the face and saying, "This is not the end."

Okay, that's a start. But what do we *do* with that faith, that belief that death is not to be feared because God can and will raise the dead? We sometimes (rightly) think of believing as the opposite of doing—like how Paul invites us into faith rather than works. But in Hebrews 11, having faith isn't the opposite of doing something. Faith in this context is actually how we do things. The whole chapter, name by name, is about people who *did things by faith*.

Faith That Moves (or Stays)

The first thing we do by faith has to do with how we *move*. "By faith Abraham, being called to go out to a place that he was about to receive as his inheritance, obeyed—and he went out even though he didn't know where he was going. By faith he settled like a foreigner in the Promised Land; he lived in tents along with Isaac and Jacob, who were fellow heirs with him of the same promise" (Heb 11:8-9). Abraham did two things. He *moved*, and he *stayed*. Not a contradiction. The act of faith in front of us might be one or the other, depending on the occasion. Sometimes God calls us to go, and even though we don't know where we're going, we go. Sometimes God calls us to stay, and even though where we are doesn't look all that appealing, we stay.

Sometimes we go. Leave your father's house, God tells Abraham in Genesis 12. Go away from what's comfortable, from what's familiar, from what's desirable, from what makes sense to those who don't know *this* place isn't *the* place.

Sometimes we stay. It's not active (go) versus passive (stay). Staying takes a lot of work—stay in that job, stay in that relationship, stay on that journey. Stay in this life. I want to get out of here. But God calls me to stay, and he keeps me alive while I'm here just like he kept the patriarchs alive in the land even when they didn't own it like their great-great-grandkids would. But notice how it says they stayed in tents. They stayed like foreigners. Do we invest in where we are, because this is where God has put us? Absolutely. But do we treat our current locations and situations as though they are the final destination? Absolutely not.

Do I treat my job, for example, as my fundamental source of life and meaning? I'm not going to change jobs every other week for the rest of my career, so to check my heart I need a micro-level version of going. Maybe I keep my job, but my responsibilities change. I train someone else to do that part of the job that I've held too tightly. I delegate responsibility in areas that I find particularly tempting as sources of meaning and identity and fulfillment. My annual review includes a "start-stop-keep" conversation—what things in my job description need to stay the way they are and what things need to change? Last time through this process I told my boss, "You can take anything off this list you want. Except for teaching hermeneutics. You can have that class when you pry it from my cold, dead fingers." I was joking, of course. Maybe. Or maybe I am holding on too tightly to something that has become a source of life for me, and I might need to give it up.

What about my relationships? I know that God has called me to *stay* by faith with Annie and our kids. But being a dad, for example, is a significant identity shaper, and so I know I'm tempted to find too much of my life (or lack thereof) in those relationships as they currently stand. My kids grow and change, and so my relationship to them grows and changes as well. This is God's grace, right? If I build myself a pedestal on account of being the world's greatest dad, my kids are sinners standing by to keep me humble. If I dig myself into a bottomless pit on account of being the world's worst dad, my kids are beloved children of God, made in his image, and they can become what he wants them to become despite my failures. Either way, their becoming something tomorrow that they aren't today is part of how God keeps me from finding too much of myself in them. The relational dynamic itself constantly moves because the people with whom I am in relationship are moving even if I'm trying not to.

Let the ectopic analogy do its real work here, reversed though the positions may be: a parent who needs to receive life from a child will suck the life right out of a child. My teenage son is no more equipped to fully enliven me than a fallopian tube is to fully enliven an unborn baby. Me trying to live vicariously through him is going to kill us both. So by faith I *stay* with my family, but as my kids grow and change, my relationship to them grows and changes as well. When they develop interests I don't share, when they say hurtful things to me, when they move away, when they don't follow in my professional steps—all these are opportunities to check *my* heart to see whether I have been seeking life where it would not be found or whether I have walked by faith in the God who keeps me alive no matter how my kids turn out.

The simplest way to see whether we are living by faith in God and not in these other things is to leave them. But that's not always what God calls us to do. Sometimes he calls us to stay in them, and in those instances the occasional fast, the occasional delegation, the occasional change can be just the heart check we need to stay and stay faithful.

Faith That Speaks

People of faith do a lot of talking. This isn't about sharing the gospel, witnessing, giving our testimony, that sort of thing—as important as those things are. This is Hebrews, which means when we talk about talking, the first thing we say is that *God speaks*. It's as true in Hebrews 11 as it is for the rest of Hebrews. The endgame of faith, in fact, is that people who live by faith receive a divine commendation (Heb 11:2). Abel is commended by God as righteous (Heb 11:4). Enoch was commended by God as pleasing to him (Heb 11:5). And at the end of the chapter, we find out that every single person named in the hall of faith is publicly commended by God for their faith (Heb 11:39). So God speaks—but in this instance, God is actually responding to people who have already spoken. I mean, they said some things, and he said some things in reply. What he said probably went something like, "Well done, good and faithful servant." But what did they say that prompted such commendation?

First: I see people of faith in Hebrews 11 speaking truth about the present. The world is not the way it's supposed to be, and we should pursue it being the way it's supposed to be while remaining continuously aware of the fact that God and God alone will accomplish that end. So, for example, look at Hebrews 11:13. When God's people stayed *in the land that had been promised to them*, they "confessed that they were foreigners and strangers in the land" (Heb 11:13). When Abraham was looking for burial grounds for Sarah, he self-identified as a "resident alien and stranger" to the Hittites who owned the land he wanted to use (Gen 23:4). That's very interesting. Abraham is living in the land that was promised to him, and he knows it. He knows that one day, his family will no longer be ectopic in that very location. But he doesn't try to control how or when that will happen. In that moment, he calls himself a foreigner to those currently in control of that land—and yet, he wants to purchase a piece of that land, to put a stake in the ground that says, "I'm not leaving." Faith isn't laziness or apathy. It isn't standing still, doing nothing, assuming that God will do whatever God will do, full stop. But faith is recognizing that ultimate outcomes, both in terms of timing and method, are up to God.

Second: faithful people in Hebrews 11 spoke truth about the future. Isaac and Jacob spoke blessings over their children and grandchildren—blessings that would only come long after they themselves were dead. Joseph spoke of the exodus, an event that took place centuries after his death. Rahab spoke welcome to the two spies, knowing that their success would be her people's demise.

Faith looks at our own lifespans and says, "This is not all there is." We planted a maple tree in our front yard this past weekend. We planted it there because we want it to shade the southeastern corner of our house. Annie and I will be dead and gone long before that tree grows tall and wide enough to do what we want it to do. Planting that tree is an act of faith—faith that our children, or someone else's children, will live to enjoy that shade.

For many of us, particularly those of us in suburban environments, the tangibility of multigenerational projects has faded. Our neighborhoods didn't exist two generations ago. The only trees on our property older than us are the ones that didn't get cut down when the developer came through. Our vehicles, our appliances, our clothing, our tools, our toys—landfill-bound by the end of the decade, at best.

I get that some things aren't going to be multigenerational. I'm not writing this book on my grandmother's typewriter. But the life of faith looks for opportunities to build things and grow things that will last beyond our own short lifespans, both because it is good for our grandchildren to inherit something and because it is good for us to leave them something to inherit (Prov 13:22).

Whatever we do, we ought to do it in such a way that the next generation is blessed rather than cursed. Whoever originally installed the sprinkler system at my house didn't know about this. Whoever planted a maple tree in the south*west* corner of my house did. It's big, it's beautiful, and we couldn't live on that end of the house in the summertime without it.

Every time I build something, I should wonder how to build it in such a way as to last for generations. Every time I plant something. Every time I write something. It's not about leaving a legacy. I have no idea who planted that old maple tree, so I'm hardly uplifting their legacy in telling this story. It's about the blessing to the future generation, not the reputation of the present or past generation. It's about faith, about trusting that God's work in the world goes beyond me, about expressing confidence that he will finish what he started even if I'm not around to see it. And of course, if God is the one who raises the dead, I will be around to see it. Not to see that specific maple tree, or that specific house, or that specific product. But to see the renewal of all things, to see the world precisely as it's supposed to be.

Faith That Sees

"We do not see all things subjected to him" (Heb 2:8). The world is obviously not being stewarded by humanity as God intended it to be, because Jesus obviously has not yet fully consummated his kingdom the way he one day will. Good things are coming, but we do not yet see them. "Faith is confidence regarding things hoped for, conviction regarding things not seen" (Heb 11:1). There's a lot we don't see. But what *do* we see?

First: We see what is not (yet?) visible. "By faith Noah, having been warned about things not yet seen, out of reverence built an ark" (Heb 11:7). "By faith Abraham . . . looked expectantly toward the city with foundations" (Heb 11:8-10). "By faith Moses . . . persevered, not fearing the king's anger, but rather seeing him who is invisible" (Heb 11:24-27). Faith is standing in my front yard, closing my eyes, and seeing not just the maple tree that already shades the southwestern corner of the house but also the maple tree that will someday shade the southeastern corner. Faith sees the future.

This isn't just positive thinking. Faith sees not optimistically but theologically. God will set the world to rights in the end. Not hopefully. Not probably. Absolutely. So, even my seeing that maple tree isn't quite right, because I have no guarantee that it will survive. Wind, drought, pest, sun, cold, fire—all these things, whether I want them to or not, can render my faith invalid. It's still an act of faith to plant and water and care for that tree, as long as it's an expression of multigenerational thinking more than it is about that one specific object.

In Hebrews 11, the invisible objects of our sight are *promises*, not *possibles*, and so to live by faith, I have to know what those promises are. "God spoke." God spoke, first, to the fathers in the prophets (Heb 1:1). He spoke, second, to us in his Son (Heb 1:2). But it isn't just that he spoke back then.

> Make sure you don't reject the one who speaks! For if they [those who were at Mount Sinai] didn't escape when he warned them on earth, how much less will we escape if we reject the one who warns us from heaven. Back then his voice shook the earth, but now he promises: "Once more I will shake not only the earth but also heaven"—now, this "once more" indicates the removal of things shaken just like they were created, so that what is unshaken may remain. (Heb 12:25-27)

God is speaking in his Son, and the echoes of that speech have not yet had their full effect. As Mount Sinai shook at the sound of God's voice, so now all of creation shakes and is being shaken. It's not that God might, someday, do something about everything that ails us. It's that he already has. "In *these last days* he has spoken in his Son," says Hebrews 1:2. We're in the last days already—we are those "on whom the end of the ages has come," as Paul says (1 Cor 10:11).

Here's an analogy for this: One of my favorite sports writers, Gregg Easterbrook, a.k.a. Tuesday Morning Quarterback, had a particular shtick in which, toward the end of an NFL game, he would see the losing team do something that amounted to throwing in the towel—usually their offense kicking a field goal when they needed a touchdown or something like that. And when that happened, Easterbrook would say, "Tuesday Morning Quarterback wrote, 'Game over' in his notebook." The game was over. Not technically, because the clock hadn't run out. But essentially, fundamentally, as far as both parties were concerned, game over.

That's where we are in history. Game over. Not technically—"We do not (yet) see all things subjected to them" (Heb 2:9). But we're at the point where knowledgeable bookies stop taking wagers. It's *over*; we just need the clock to run out. But here the analogy breaks down, because in football, there's a clock.[4] And part of why we say "Game over" is that we can see the clock, and we know how much time is on it. Not so in real life. You and I have no idea how much time is left on the clock—whether for our own individual lives or for the world as a whole. And so faith that sees us in the waning moments of a competition wherein the final outcome has already been decided also recognizes that seeing the final destination doesn't change how little we see of the journey from here to there.

In 2007 a young private in the US Marines named Matthew Bradford stepped on an IED in Iraq and lost both his legs and both his eyes. It was five months before he stood up again, on prosthetics, a double amputee, blind in both eyes, but a few years later he was running marathons. I heard him on a podcast reflecting on what it's like to run a marathon when blind, and he said, "The miles are a lot longer when you can't see."[5] *The miles are a lot longer when you can't see.*

One of my favorite books is called *Born to Run*, by Christopher Mc-Dougall. If you haven't read it, just go right now and order it. It's amazing. One of the most amazing threads in this incredible story is about something called "persistence hunting." It's Stone Age hunting, literally. No

---

[4]My apologies to the world outside the United States, to those of you for whom *football* means a sport in which only the referee knows how much time is on the clock. That might have helped my analogy, actually. Oh well.

[5]Jocko Willink, host, *Jocko Podcast*, episode 171 (1:13:28-31). Originally aired on April 3, 2019 (https://www.youtube.com/watch?v=m5CkAJu9t8E).

gun, no spear, nothing. A group of tribesmen go out and start chasing their prey—a deer, or something like that. And as long as you can keep track of that specific animal, as long as you can track it across the ground and distinguish it from the herd, you keep chasing it. And you chase it until *it* drops dead from exhaustion. Hard to imagine, I know, even for those of us who like running. But it's real, and really hard, and here's the hardest thing about it: you don't know how long it's going to take for that animal to die. How long and how far are you going to run, and over what terrain? *You don't know.* How long is our personal journey of faith going to be until our faith becomes sight? *We don't know.* Persistence hunting isn't a sprint, for sure. It's not even a marathon, because a marathon is a predetermined distance along a predetermined path. The life of faith is a persistence hunt, because even though we know what the final destination is, and we know (or should know) a good number of tactical pieces of how we're going to arrive at that destination, there's an awful lot of unknown in between here and there. The miles are a lot longer when you can't see, and even longer when you don't know how many miles there are going to be.

The second thing we see: Especially when we can't see anything else, we look to Jesus. "We do not see all things subjected to him. But we do see Jesus" (Heb 2:8-9). "Let us run with perseverance the race set before us by looking at Jesus" (Heb 12:1-2).

What does that mean? Anything we say about Jesus so easily slips into slogans. "What would Jesus do?" But it's so much more than that. Part of it is the fact that Jesus has already done what he is inviting us to do. "Jesus, the pioneer and perfecter of faith, for the joy set before him endured the cross by despising its shame" (Heb 12:2). What are we invited to do? Look ahead to the joy of uninhibited relationship with our Father and the joy of stewarding the new creation, and endure the difficulties that life under the sun inevitably entails when we live as refugees waiting for the eternal kingdom. In other words, do exactly what he did. And the point of looking at him is, in part, to be reminded that what we have been called to do has already been accomplished.

I'm not reducing the work of Jesus to positive psychology. It's a fact that seeing someone else do something we didn't think could be done rewires our brains.[6] What we thought was impossible is now possible. Hebrews 11 reminds us that we can resist temptation—Jesus showed us it was possible. We can endure unjust suffering without taking on the victim identity—Jesus showed us that it could be done and how to do it. I can imagine all sorts of horrifying experiences that I cannot imagine enduring. But when I meet someone who endured that horror and hear their story, I realize that, yes, it is possible. It *can* be done. Hebrews 11 shows us what people can do by faith. Jesus' own story shows us what can be done by faith. That's part of what is happening here.

The other part is that Hebrews 12:2 calls Jesus not only the pioneer but also the perfecter of faith. As pioneer, he went out into uncharted territory, navigated it successfully, and then came back—and now he invites others to join him in repeating the journey that he alone knows how to complete. As perfecter, though, he isn't just the first person to find a way across the desert. He's the one who went out into the desert and built a road, dug a well, and grew an oasis. He posted signs, he printed maps, he put into place every single component required for a successful journey.[7] And having made it so we *can* complete our journeys, he then accompanies us every step of the way in order to guarantee that we *will* complete those journeys. He started things off (pioneer), and he will finish them (perfecter). "Look at Jesus" does mean, "Look at how he already did what he's asking you to do," but it also means, "Look at how he has met every possible need you could have along the way, and look at how he walks with you from start to finish."

I like Jocko Willink. Whenever someone comes up to Jocko and says, "You changed my life," he responds with, "I didn't change your life—you changed your life. You got up early, you got the workout in,

---

[6]Yoram Wind and Colin Crook, *The Power of Impossible Thinking: Transform the Business of Your Life* (Philadelphia: Wharton School Publishing, 2006), goes deep on this point.

[7]As one scholar puts it, "The way of faith is not under construction. It is open from beginning to end." Gareth L. Cockerill, *The Epistle to the Hebrews*, New International Commentary on the New Testament (Grand Rapids, MI: Eerdmans, 2012), 607.

you took ownership of your problems, you did it." That's true. People like Jocko show us what's possible, humanly speaking. They show us a better way to live; they inspire us with their example and their rhetoric and their strategic and tactical guidance. But when we look at Jesus and say, "You changed my life," he doesn't respond with, "I didn't change your life—you changed your life." When I say to Jesus, "You changed my life," he says, "That's right. I did." That doesn't mean I didn't do anything. It doesn't mean I sat on the couch and waited for Jesus to transform me and the world around me. But it does mean that Jesus, by giving me his Spirit, has changed me in ways that neither I, nor any self-help guru or motivational speaker or business coach, could ever have accomplished.

We should celebrate those who have stewarded well the talents that God has given them and produced a lot out of a little. But there's an infinite gap between making a lot out of a little and making something out of nothing. Doctors can make sick people well. Only God can make dead people live. When we look to Jesus, a man who died and now lives, we see that God is indeed the God who raises the dead. And when we look a bit closer and remember that Jesus is himself God, one with the Father, "equal in power and glory and majesty," as the creed says it, we see not only one man raised to life; we see the God-man calling and enabling the rest of his brothers and sisters to join him. Look to Jesus and see not only where we're going but how we get there.

Faith That Hears

I mentioned a bit ago that Hebrews 11, like every other part of Hebrews, is about *God speaking*. That commendation we receive from God when we walk by faith—that's the main thing. It's not empty words: it's God's invitation to life. Life eternal, life overflowing, life resurrected.

There's an amazing story hidden in Hebrews 11:35. It's the hinge between "sometimes the life of faith turns out well in the short term" (Heb 11:33-35) and "sometimes the life of faith means a pretty rough ride in this present life" (Heb 11:35-38). It says, "Others were tortured but refused to be released, so that they might receive an even better resurrection."

Put yourself in the time of Hebrews (second half of the first century AD) and then back up another two hundred years or so, the middle of the second century BC. This fellow named Antiochus Epiphanes is ruling the portion of the fragmented Greek empire that includes Judea, and he decides one day that the Jews are being too Jewish. Every other conquered people group is okay with becoming Greek—speaking Greek, thinking Greek, dressing Greek, eating Greek. But this one dinky little pocket of the empire wants to be difficult about such things, and Antiochus has had enough. So he decides to make a point in the most undiplomatic way possible. He and his soldiers head south from Syria to Jerusalem; they're going to slaughter a pig on the altar in the temple in Jerusalem as an offering to himself (Antiochus), and the Jewish people there will, on pain of torture and death, eat the sacrificial meat.

If you know your Old Testament at all, you know there are all kinds of reasons why no God-fearing Jew would ever have any part of this. Antiochus knew those reasons, and that was the point. "Be loyal to me, period. None of this faith-of-our-fathers nonsense."

Antiochus and company show up in Jerusalem, they slaughter the pig, and they line up the Jews to partake of the idolatrous meal. Among those in line are a mother and her seven sons.[8] The oldest son is brought to the front, and Antiochus says, "Eat the pork." And the son responds with, "Not a chance." So they take him aside, cut off his hands and feet and tongue, and fry him in an oversized frying pan. Cue son number two. Repeat. Son number three doesn't want to waste anyone's time—he simply stretches out his hands and says, "Get it over with. I got these from God, and he'll give them back, so let's not complicate this." Likewise sons four, five, and six.

All the while, the mother is standing there, watching this unfold, "encouraging them in their ancestral language" (2 Macc 7:21). So

---

[8]The details are found in a book called 2 Maccabees; it's in the Apocrypha, which means it's in Catholic and Orthodox Bibles but not in the Protestant Bible. I'm not treating it as sacred Scripture here, but I am treating it as a story that the author of Hebrews would have known and as a story that illustrates quite brilliantly the point the author of Hebrews is trying to make.

Antiochus (who is supposed to be the star of the show) is getting told off by each son in his turn, and those sons, instead of paying any attention to him, are conversing with their mom in a language he doesn't understand. My favorite line in the story: after six sons up and six sons down, with Antiochus being told, "You're an idiot, this isn't even about you, we and God are doing business here," by each of them in turn, and watching them talk to their mother with the sort of respect that he wanted for himself—it says he "began to feel that he was being treated with contempt" (2 Macc 7:24). Indeed. The same sort of contempt, perhaps, with which Moses viewed "being known as the son of Pharoah's daughter" (Heb 11:24).

That contempt continued when Antiochus tried to bribe the seventh son with all sorts of honors and privileges in his court, and the son responded with, "What are you waiting for? I'm not interested" (2 Macc 7:30). Like "all the treasures of Egypt" (Heb 11:26), that son saw all the glory of Antiochus. Dust and ashes, meaningless, emptiness, vanity—"compared to the surpassing greatness of knowing Christ" (Phil 3:8).

The Maccabean martyrs teach us how to *listen* by faith. They were inundated with sounds, of which the king—symbolic of all that was evil in their world—was the loudest. "Eat the pig." "Deny your God." "Forget who you were." Every sensory element in the room amplified his voice: the burning flesh of the brothers, the mocking shouts of the soldiers, the submissive Jews who stood ahead of them in the line. The noise was overwhelming—but it wasn't. One voice somehow penetrated the cacophony. Through the clamor, through the chaos, somehow, the brothers heard their mother speak. And look what she says! She tells them to remember God's laws (2 Macc 7:6, 23). She tells them to remain faithful even when they are surrounded by unfaithfulness (2 Macc 7:20-22). She tells them that God, not Antiochus, is the one who gives and takes away life (2 Macc 7:23, 28). She plays this one note, again and again, and her sons echo it back to her: God is the giver of life. God gave us life in the first place, and if we remain faithful in this moment, he will give it back to us again. Over and over, they repeat the mantra: "The King of the world will raise us up to an everlasting renewal of life" (2 Macc 7:9; similarly 2 Macc 7:11, 14, 23, 29, 36). New hands, new feet, new tongues, new life—the better resurrection.

What fear need there be of dying if we shall be raised? This is the fundamental question of Hebrews 11. And the answer that faith gives, and thereby merits God's commendation in return, is this: the judgment by sinners is of no account, even if it means death, for the one who gave us life in the beginning, and keeps us alive for as long as he wishes, is the one who will raise us once again to life *en topos*—no longer out of place but in place, in him, never to die again.

Study Questions

1. Have you ever taken a leap of faith? How long did it take to land?

2. What exactly do you believe about God that makes him worth believing in? List a few things.

3. We have a God who raises the dead. What situation are you currently in that you need to believe in *that* God?

4. How might God be calling you to *go* or to *stay* in your current life season?

5. What race are you running right now that you can't see the finish line, and you don't know how far away the finish line is? How do you need to look to Jesus in the midst of that race?

6. What do you need to hear (by faith) God speak in your current season of life?

15

FEELING OUT OF PLACE?

BRENÉ BROWN LIKES TO ASK her podcast guests about the worst advice they've ever received. I doubt I'll ever have the privilege of being on her show, but if I did and she asked me this question, I'd probably have to go back to some of the things I heard, as a single person, about preparing for marriage. You know the classic line: the primary thing we do, as singles, is "save ourselves for marriage." What do single people do? Nothing, apparently, because the primary thing they hear from their Christian communities is that they need to devote themselves fully to *not* doing the one thing that married people do.

There's a whole lot of what people are now calling "purity culture" in what I'm targeting here. A lot of "Don't have sex until your wedding night, and then your marriage will be awesome." A lot of "I'm so sorry you're twenty-seven and still single; that must be hard for you." A lot of "What more could a father want for his daughter than for her to transfer her allegiance from him to some other guy?" A whole lot of nonsense. A whole lot of—and here's the key—a whole lot of assuming that *life* means *married* life, and it's all just sitting back and waiting until we become fully human in our marital union.

I'm married. Presumably you know that already, if you've been reading this book. But what I want to say here is for both those who are married and those who are single, because both have been invited to receive the ectopic life of Jesus—which implies, already, that both are ectopic. Both single and married alike need to receive life from outside, and therefore, according to Hebrews, both need (among other things) to *stay* by faith. For some, until death do us part, staying by faith means staying married. For others, staying by faith means right now, and might mean for the duration, staying single.

I want first to offer a word to those who are single. The word is this: *fast*. Not fast as in the opposite of *slow* but fast as in the opposite of *feast*. As in, the spiritual discipline of giving up a good thing now in order to imbibe more fully of a better thing later. We fast from food in order to remember that we live not by bread alone but by the sustenance of God's Word. We fast from social media during Lent to remember that history is in the hands of God and not public opinion. We fast from good things for the sake of better things.

Some of you are tempted to drop this book and run right now because you think you know where this is going. You think I'm about to say that singleness is a fast in anticipation of the feast that is marriage. But I'm not. I'm not going to say that singleness is about saving yourself for marriage, because that's not what the Bible says about singleness or marriage. What the Bible actually says is this: Marriage is an image, a "shadowy illustration," to use Hebrews' term, of the greater reality that is the relationship between Christ and his church (Eph 5:22-33). Recall the glorious scene in Revelation 19 and Revelation 21 of the "marriage supper" of the Lamb (Rev 19:9). *That's* the feast. Eternity as his bride, eternity in unceasing intimacy with him—*that's* the better thing. *That's* what you're "saving yourself" for. Singleness is a fast in preparation for an eternal feast.

Paul says that to be *single* is to have a *single* focus in life: "undistracted devotion to the Lord" (1 Cor 7:35). If you've fasted, you know what that feels like: your whole body and mind bent in one direction, resisting whatever it is you're fasting from and opening yourself up to be filled by something else. Fasting is integrating, because it forces our whole selves to get on the same page. That's singleness. Forget the absurd rhetoric of singles as half-persons, somehow enduring life without that person who completes them. In Paul's way of thinking, a single person can be more internally whole than a married person, because a single person is not distracted by the good thing now from the better thing later (1 Cor 7:32-34).

I'm not bashing marriage. It's not hating on marriage to say that being single holds potential for holiness that marriage doesn't. Paul isn't being antimarriage when he says that marriage *isn't* the fullness of human experience, any more than he is being antisports when he says that the crowns of victorious athletes aren't going to last forever (1 Cor 9:25). Every good thing, we either scorn it as too little, as we often do with singleness, or we idolize it as too much, as we often do with marriage. We make it the feast.

Marriage, that incredible God-given union of a man and a woman. What is it? It's not the feast. It's not the fast. It's the snack. I know—not our standard biblical imagery for marriage. I don't mean the snack that ruins your appetite, the bag of candy sneaked out of the cupboard right before dinner. At least, it wasn't designed to be that kind of snack. I think it is for some of us. But marriage *as it should be* isn't that kind of snack. Marriage is more like the samples at Baskin Robbins, like the spoonful of soup that the cook samples before filling up the bowls, like the piece of fudge that doesn't fit on the tray but still needs to be eaten. It's the same food as the feast, but only a tiny fraction of it, not nearly enough to satisfy.

Two people are waiting for a feast. One of them has been snacking, the other has been fasting. The one who has been fasting is hungrier, and that is to their advantage. The one who has been snacking has a slightly better idea of what the feast is going to taste like, and that too is to their advantage. But both of them have been called to *stay* by faith, to *wait* by faith for the fullness of life that is yet to come.

When you feel trapped in your marriage—stay.[1] Not because your marriage will last for eternity, because it won't. Stay because your marriage,

---

[1] Feeling trapped in your marriage on account of unmet expectations and being trapped in your marriage because of abuse are not the same thing. To be clear: in this context I'm talking about unmet expectations.

your union with another human being, is an image of the true and eternal union that we will experience with Christ as his bride (Eph 5:31-32). When marriage functions as it was designed to function, it is a taste of eternity. And so as you *stay* by faith, you also *speak* by faith. You, by your faithfulness, say, "Here is a glimpse into what eternal union with Christ looks like." When you stay, you speak to the rest of us; you tell us that the snack is good, and how much better must be the feast. That is how you, as a married person, receive the life of Christ and give that life to the rest of us.

Likewise, when you feel trapped in your singleness—stay. It's a little different, isn't it? A married person has made a lifelong covenant promise to stay. If you're single, you haven't necessarily made a promise like that. God might someday call you to *move*. He might summon you out of your current position. But for now, stay. Once again, *stay* by faith so that you can also *speak* by faith. Speak to us. Tell us that there is a feast coming and that you refuse to spoil your appetite with hors d'oeuvres. Next time someone says, "I'm sorry you haven't found anyone yet," say, "Before I leave this life, I may taste of that snack, but I was never going to be satiated by it anyway. My life is hidden with Christ in God, not in earthly marriage." When you stay, you speak: you tell us that there is a feast, and when it comes, no one will remember the appetizer anyway. That is how you, as a single person, receive the life of Christ and give that life to the rest of us.

Study Questions

1. What's the worst advice you've ever received?

2. Have you felt pressured to see marriage as the feast, as the ultimate source of life? How has that affected your experience of either marriage, singleness, or both?

3. What does "staying" by faith look like for you right now, particularly in your familial context?

16

LOVE IN A LIFELESS WORLD

LOVE. I NEED A GOOD STORY HERE, RIGHT? In Christian contexts, we go to Jesus—"This is love, not that we loved God, but that he loved us, and sent his Son to be an atoning sacrifice for our sins" (1 Jn 4:10). But God's love started way before that. Israel? Before that. Abraham? Keep going. Creation? Nope, not even then. God loved and was love personified even before there was anything other than himself to love in the first place. How is that possible? So glad you asked.

The most basic Christian doctrine—and when I say *basic* I mean "most foundational to all the other doctrines" *and* "most uniquely Christian"—is the doctrine of the Trinity. The doctrine of the Trinity can be summarized by saying that there is one God who exists eternally as three persons (Father, Son, Spirit), who are individually and collectively one and the same God. You can't have a Father without a Son, you can't have a Son without a Father, and you can't have either without the Spirit, who binds them together in love. That's right: in *love*. If you scrunch up your brain for a second and try to ponder the question, "What was God doing before he made everything else?" you end up saying something like, "He was being Father, Son, and Spirit, which means perfect unity and perfect freedom and perfect love."

Here's why that matters: God, before there was anything else besides God, wasn't bored. He wasn't lonely. He was absolutely content. But neither was he self-absorbed, in the way that you and I can get self-absorbed when we are isolated from everyone else. So when he created us, he didn't create us out of necessity, as though he really wanted to express his love but had spent all eternity up to that point being unable to do so. Nor did he change who he was after he created us, like a new parent who realizes there's a lot about their lifestyle that is going to give way to this ridiculously needy addition to their household. He was already perfectly happy, perfectly self-expressed in the love of the Father for the Son, the Son for the Spirit, and so on.[1]

So why create us at all? Because he *wanted* (not *needed*) to see that love overflow from himself into something else. Maybe you've heard that God created us so we could glorify him. True in a sense, but more fundamentally he created us so that he could love us. Imagine that: the reason you and I exist is to be recipients (and conduits) of God's love that overflows from the love that's already there between Father, Son, and Spirit. This is the original love story: that God, as Father, Son, and Spirit, wanted to share his love with us, and the rest is history.

That history isn't us riding off into the sunset, though. It's us getting to work. It's our being the creaturely recipients of God's love that he intended us to be. And God's love is infinite. It can't be contained in me, or you, or all of us put together. It has to overflow. It has to come out of us just like it came into us, and that means we become conduits of God's love to others, not just containers into which God's love has come. Isn't that something? The previous part of this book was about *faith*, because faith is how we survive our ectopic condition—it's how we find life in the first place. That's Hebrews 11. *Love* is what we do with that life once we've found it. That's Hebrews 13.

Love and Worship

"Let us worship God acceptably, with reverent awe, because he is a consuming fire" (Heb 12:28-29): it's the climactic pronouncement of the entire sermon. If the God whose presence tears Mount Sinai apart,

---

[1]If you want to meditate more deeply on God as Trinity and God as love, I can't recommend strongly enough Michael Reeves's *Delighting in the Trinity* (Downers Grove, IL: IVP Academic, 2012).

whose covenant oaths can never be revoked, whose holiness prohibits
any sin or blemish from getting too close—if *that* God says, "Come near,
come in, come be with me," we are going to want to do that on his terms,
not ours. So we worship *acceptably*.[2] If you don't come to Hebrews 13
ready to take entrance into God's presence seriously, you're not ready for
this chapter. If you treat following Jesus into the holiest of all holy places
like following your date to the buffet line, you're not ready for this
chapter. Go back and read the first three parts of this book, or, better yet,
go back and read Hebrews. Our God is a consuming fire, and that means
we tread lightly when we get close.

When you picture worshiping "with reverent awe," you probably envision either a high-church liturgy (reverence = formality) or a Bethel
concert (reverence = passion). I'm reasonably certain that Scripture encourages both. "Praise God in his sanctuary. . . . Praise him with timbrel
and dancing!" (Ps 150:1, 4). "Be still, and know that I am God" (Ps 46:10).
But what comes after "worship God acceptably" (Heb 12:28-29) isn't the
physical posture of the worshiper or the aura of the worship gathering.
It's *love*. Love for one another as brothers and sisters (Heb 13:1). Love for
strangers and foreigners (Heb 13:2). Love for those in prison and those
who are being mistreated (Heb 13:3). Love for marriage—both yours and
everyone else's (Heb 13:4). *Not* love for money (Heb 13:5). "Let brotherly
love remain. Do not neglect hospitality, because through hospitality
some have unknowingly welcomed angels. Remember those who are
imprisoned, since you have been imprisoned as well, and remember
those who are being mistreated, since you too have suffered bodily
injury" (Heb 13:1-3). The first sentence overshadows the rest. The quint-
essential action toward other people prompted by reverent awe for God
is love. And the specific command that love "remain" reminds us of what
was just said a couple of lines earlier: that we are receiving a kingdom

---

[2]This text is not about what we commonly call "worship style." And yet, our inability to
take real worship seriously can't help but be related to the too common practice of treating
musical worship as a choose-your-own-adventure story. "Worship however you feel led."
"We like the worship here." This sort of nonsense has got to stop. If we call an activity
worship and then tell people that they are free to choose their own variety of that activity,
we are idolaters. Worship is done on God's terms and no others.

that "remains" (Heb 12:27). Love is a fitting action for those who already inhabit and will one day receive such a kingdom.

It really shouldn't surprise us that love is how we worship. James says something similar in his letter: "With our tongues we praise God, and with our tongues we curse people made in his likeness. Out of the same mouth come praise and cursing. This should not be!" (Jas 3:9-10). The prophets are likewise adamant: "I hate, I despise your religious festivals; your assemblies are a stench to me. . . . Away with the noise of your songs! I will not listen to the music of your harps. But let justice roll on like a river, righteousness like a never-failing stream!" (Amos 5:21, 23-24 NIV). "Stop bringing meaningless offerings! . . . I cannot bear your worthless assemblies. . . . Take your evil deeds out of my sight; stop doing wrong. Learn to do right; seek justice. Defend the oppressed" (Is 1:13, 16-17 NIV). Need I say more? It's one of the most basic teachings of the Bible and one of the easiest for us to forget: you can't love God and hate your brother or sister. "If anyone has material goods and sees their brother or sister in need and closes their heart toward that person, how could God's love be in them?!" (1 Jn 3:17).

Interesting little Greek note here: the word we translate as "hospitality" (Heb 13:2) is a combination of two words: *philos* and *xenos*. You've heard of Philadelphia, which is *philos* plus *adelphos*. *Philos* means "love," and *adelphos* means "brother" (or sibling), so Philadelphia is the city of "brotherly love," and that's what's commanded in Hebrews 13:1—let *philadelphia* remain. You've also heard of xenophobia, *xenos* plus *phobia*, which means "fear of strangers." So now put *philos* in front of *xenos*, which is the word we have here, *philoxenia*, and you get "love of strangers." That's what hospitality is. It's love of strangers. So let love remain. Love those who are close, who are insiders, who are like you, but don't forget about those who are not insiders, those who are unlike you: make sure you have some *philoxenia* along with your *philadelphia*.[3]

---

[3]There's something rather odd tucked into these verses. How do I know whether I've "unknowingly welcomed angels"? I can't say that I've got a great answer to that question, and neither does anyone else, if a scan of the scholarly literature is any indication. For a

Love for those who are like you, love for those who are not. Then love for those who are suffering (Heb 13:3). Some from the first audience of Hebrews had suffered on account of their faith; that suffering included shame, imprisonment, and confiscation of property (Heb 10:32-34). They, like Moses and others, had endured mistreatment for the sake of Christ (Heb 11:25, 37), and now they are reminded that such experiences are to be expected and to be faithfully endured by those who follow Jesus. But beyond our own experience of such difficulties, we are also called to stand with others who are experiencing them. Jesus himself no longer endures those pains, but he remains close to those who do—that's how love and life overflow from him to us and from us to others.

Love and Marriage

"Marriage? Let it be honored by all, and let the marriage bed remain undefiled, because God will judge the immoral or adulterous person" (Heb 13:4). The next two commands—marriage and money—relate to two of the major arenas in which we are called to imitate Jesus by seeking the good of others rather than ourselves. They are petri dishes for either self-denial or self-worship, and if our worship is already spoken for, we'll deny ourselves. Honoring marriage could imply a lot of things. I honor my marriage when I treat my spouse a certain way. I also honor someone else's marriage when I treat another married person a certain way. So whether or not I am married, I still honor marriage *at least* every time I interact with a married person. (I'm assuming we all have at least one person in our lives who fits that description.) So this covers a *lot* of ground! How I act toward my wife in private, how I act toward her in public, how I speak of her when she's not there. How I treat married persons of the opposite biological sex—would I act like that if their spouse were in the room? How I speak and think about marriage in

---

summary of options see Harold W. Attridge, *The Epistle to the Hebrews: A Commentary*, Hermeneia (Philadelphia: Fortress, 1989), 386. One thing I do find interesting is that angels have been off the table for a few chapters in Hebrews, but way back in Heb 1–2 we were talking about angels as those who serve us (Heb 1:14). Perhaps there's something here about loving and serving those who are of lower sociological status than ourselves?

general (this includes rejecting the idolization of marriage I mentioned back in chapter fifteen). The list goes on—to honor marriage means a great many things. But the reasoning for the command in this context means that Hebrews has some specific features of marital honor in mind. *God will judge the immoral or adulterous person.*

Three angles on this. First, immorality and adultery technically refer to sexual activity outside marriage, and sexual activity outside *your* marriage, respectively. So I've mentioned the way you talk about your spouse in your spouse's absence as a way of honoring marriage, but that isn't technically what's in view here (though it certainly may be a step on the road toward what is in view). But *why*? I mean, teenagers, unmarried adults, and unhappily married adults the world over want to know, really, compellingly, *why* does God prohibit sexual activity outside marriage? There's one thing worth saying here that I don't think gets said often enough, and it's this: sexual intercourse is a covenant reenactment ceremony. "This is my body, given for you." Covenant reenactments are about *embodied oneness.* All five senses engaged, connectivity uninhibited by distance or distraction, the only thing happening in the world right now is *this.* What standing on the mountain and reading Deuteronomy does for Israel, what participation in the Lord's Supper does for the church, sex does for a marriage. Husband and wife come together and say, "The covenant promises we have made with each other continue to define who we are, and what God has brought together, let no one separate." Of course, there's more to sex than this, but there isn't less. Sexual intercourse without a covenant to reenact isn't, can't be, sex as God designed it.

Second, one scholar points out that the warning against illicit sexual activity may have been prompted by the circumstances outlined in the preceding commands.[4] Hospitality means having people in your home, but don't let that outreach destroy your home by letting someone else come between you and your spouse. Having one spouse in prison could certainly open the door to adultery! I don't speak lightly of this. Marital

---

[4]Craig R. Koester, *Hebrews: A New Translation with Introduction and Commentary,* Anchor Bible 36 (New York: Doubleday, 2001), 565.

faithfulness in absentia is no easy thing. Under circumstances that could more easily lead to such behavior, not to mention a cultural context that permitted just about any sexual activity under the sun (an increasingly familiar scenario in our own context), Hebrews wanted to be very clear: no excuses. God does not mess around with such things.

That's the third thing—God will judge. Why here, why now, why in Hebrews 13 are we talking about this? Because Hebrews is about a God who is very close. And proximity to him requires purity. Not external, physical purity, as though we can't come to him without taking a shower. Internal purity—purity of the conscience. "The blood of Christ, who by the eternal Spirit offered himself blameless to God, will cleanse our consciences from actions that lead to death so that we can serve the living God" (Heb 9:14). We can't stain our consciences with immorality and then waltz on in to God's presence.

This isn't the time for a comprehensive look at sexuality in the Bible, but here's one thing you need to know: sex is sacred. Sex is *holy*. There are some weird ideas out there about the intersection of sex and the sacred, and I'm not going to follow that rabbit hole all the way down, but we need to understand at least a little bit of how this works.

In Old Testament terms, there are holy things and there are common things. Holy things are set apart for particular activities.[5] You only use *that* bowl for *this* ritual. Common things are just plain old things. You can use *that* bowl for everyday activities that are not part of any particular ritual. Holy things and common things don't mix. It is important to realize, though, that *holy* doesn't mean "sinless," and *common* doesn't mean "sinful." The bowl you use for your breakfast? It's common. That doesn't mean there's something wrong with it. It just means it hasn't been set apart by God for one specific activity. Most of the things Israel possessed would have been considered common.

So far, the distinction isn't about right and wrong. But it becomes about right and wrong when you blur the categories. When you use

---

[5]One dictionary helpfully defines the Hebrew word *qdš* ("holy") as "withheld from ordinary use." Jackie Naudé, "קדשׁ," *New International Dictionary of Old Testament Theology and Exegesis*, ed. Willem A. VanGemeren (Grand Rapids, MI: Zondervan, 1997), 3:877.

something common when you should have used something that was holy. Or, as was more often the case, when you used something holy when you should have used something common, or used something holy as though it were common. This is what the Bible means when it says you've "profaned" something. You've taken something that has been set apart and acted like it's no big deal, nothing special. Israel was constantly getting in trouble for profaning God's name—treating God's name like it wasn't anything special, or doing things "in his name" that were clearly contrary to the character that his name represented (such as sacrificing their children in his name [Lev 18:21], or swearing falsely in his name [Lev 19:12]).[6] The big one was when Israel got taken out of their land despite God's promises to give them that land—so the other nations said, "That god isn't anything special." When that happened, God said, "You profaned my holy name wherever you went among the other nations" (Ezek 36:20-23).

What's this got to do with marriage and sex? Sexual activity is set apart. It's sacred. My body belongs to my wife and to no other. Her body belongs to me and to no other. So if some other person desires sexual fulfillment, they're not going to get it from one of us. It's like a child reaching for one of the sacred vessels in the temple in order to put their toys in it and being told, "That's not what that's for." My body is not available for anyone's sexual satisfaction except for my wife's. To everyone else: *that's not what that's for.*

By the way—this applies beyond simply having intercourse with someone to whom you are not married. Sexual humor treats sex as no big deal. Sexual language—what is properly called *profanity*—treats sex as a common or even dirty thing. Sexual entertainment treats sex as demeaning, violent, or purely economic. These are all profane acts; they are all ways of *dis*honoring marriage and defiling what God considers holy. How do you think he's going to respond to that? God hasn't

---

[6]For what it means to treat God's name inappropriately ("in vain," as many of our Bibles put it in the Ten Commandments texts), see Carmen J. Imes, *Bearing YHWH's Name at Sinai: A Reexamination of the Name Command of the Decalogue,* Bulletin for Biblical Research, Supplements 19 (University Park, PA: Eisenbrauns, 2018).

changed. Swift and terrible judgment is God's unrelenting response to those who profane what he has pronounced sacred.

Love and Money

"Love of money? Leave no place for it by being content with what is available to you, because God himself says to you, 'I will never leave you or forsake you,' and therefore we respond by saying, 'the Lord is my helper; I will not be afraid—what can people do to me?'" (Heb 13:5-6). Enough about sex. How about money? Look at Hebrews 13:5-6. Don't love money—seems pretty obvious from a biblical perspective. But what's fascinating about this particular jab at greed is the reason for it. Don't love money, *because God speaks*. And no surprise, the thing he speaks is a quotation from the Old Testament—Deuteronomy 31:6. What does God say? "I will never leave you or forsake you." Wholehearted pursuit of money is the same as wholehearted pursuit of anything else. It's prompted by a perceived lack of something, and not just the thing you're pursuing but whatever it is that you think that thing will bring you. No one cares inherently about numbers on an account, or pieces of paper with faces on it, or stamped metal. We care about money because money means security, safety, fulfillment of desires, accomplishment, attractiveness. And Hebrews says, "Don't pursue money like that," because God says, "I'm not going anywhere. I've got you covered." When we let understandable fear (being impoverished isn't fun) turn into obsession with economic security, we're not listening to God speak.

Now this is interesting: It isn't just, "Don't love money, because God said something that should show us that we don't need to love money." God says something, and then what? For the first time in Hebrews, the speaker of Scripture is . . . us. You and me. We get in on the conversation. God says, "I will never leave you or forsake you" (Deut 31:6), and we respond with, "The Lord is my helper; I will not be afraid—what can people do to me?" (Ps 118:6-7). Struggling with fears about money? You know you are. (If you're not, it's worth asking, Why not? Is it because you've been financially successful? Or is it because you know that God will never leave you or forsake you?) Part of the right response to financial fears is to speak the truths of Scripture. But notice that it isn't merely reciting a verse like a mantra to make ourselves feel better. It's being part of a dialogue. It's *listening* to what God says to you, and then, in response, *speaking* God's words back to him.[7] You can't say your part if you haven't first heard his.

Notice that Hebrews 13:5 doesn't simply say, "Don't love money." It says, "Let love of money have no place—and the way to accomplish that is to be content with what you have." That contentment, Hebrews 13:6 goes on to say, is possible because of what God has said ("I will never leave you or forsake you"), and it is expressed by what we say ("The Lord is my helper; I will not be afraid—what can people do to me?"). So the sequence goes like this: God speaks → we speak → we act.

But what exactly does contentment look like? Does it mean apathy, never seeking advancement, staying exactly where you are until you die? I think not. It doesn't say *stay* where you are; it says *be content with* where you are. God invites us to increase, grow, build, create, cultivate. But discontent is the great motivator of change, is it not? How do we move if we are not dissatisfied with where we are? Here are a couple of thoughts, knowing that there's much more that could be said.

First, as is so often the case, we have to ask the *why* question. *Why do I desire to possess more than I currently do?* Of course, part of the issue is in the word *possess*. Debt is slavery—that we know well. But so is ownership. Only in stewardship—it all belongs to someone else; we are merely managers for a season—is freedom found.[8] Why do I want *more*? I can think of four possible motivations.

Contestant number one: I would be more content if I had more money. Nope. Not biblical. Wealth as the mechanism of contentment is a mirage. There's certainly such thing as "enough money to do some things and avoid other things." The temptation here is to want enough

---

[7] I'm reminded of what John Goldingay (my Psalms professor in seminary) said: "The Psalms are both God's words to us and our words to God."

[8] I have a "Theology of Development" document someone gave me years ago, and though unfortunately I don't know where it originated, it is worth quoting here: "We are on a journey from the bondage of ownership to the freedom of the faithful steward." You can also check out my podcast, *Extreme Stewardship*, for more reflections on this point.

money that I won't need faith anymore. But there's only one way to get beyond the need for faith, and that's the return and reign of Jesus and my own resurrection and coming face to face with God himself. Money is going to look pretty insignificant on that day, don't you think?

Contestant number two: I would provide better for my family if I had more money. Maybe. I've gone to Annie more than once and said, "I want to make more money for your sake." And sometimes she says, "We're fine; we'd rather have you home more," and sometimes she says, "Yeah, that would be really helpful; let's talk details." I also have to discern whether my desire to be a "better provider" is based on what would be good for them or what would feel good to me. When I see a nine-year-old rolling up to baseball practice with a thousand dollars in equipment but the whole season goes by without Mom or Dad making an appearance, I have to wonder.

Contestant number three: I would be more generous if I had more money. Maybe. Am I already generous? If I want to get to a six-figure income because "then I can afford to be generous," I don't understand generosity. Just about everyone I know who is wealthy and generous used to be poor and generous. They loved friend and stranger alike when their pockets were empty, and they have continued to do so now that their pockets are full.

Contestant number four: It would reflect better on my employer if I had more money. Again: maybe. My boss once told me that our salaries were an embarrassment to him, because employee compensation communicates things about the health of the company. So if I want my employer to succeed—and oh, by the way, that success would probably lead to a pay raise—great. My dad used to say that the job of every employee is to make the boss look good. But even then, my boss is not ultimately Great Northern University. It is Jesus Christ, and his standard of success is often different from mine. Maybe I make him look good by navigating financial success in a particular way (notice that "I make him look good by *achieving* financial success" is never the plan), or maybe I make him look good by navigating financial failure in a particular way.

The question, Why do I want *more*? has a range of possible answers. Some are always wrong, and others are sometimes right, sometimes wrong. That's how wisdom works. But let's say I am reasonably confident that my motivations are properly aligned—I'm pursuing additional financial resources not for my own sake but for others' sake, for the kingdom's sake. So I've answered the "Why do I want more money?" question correctly. That's a good start but hardly a guarantee that I am perfectly navigating the tension between contentment and advancement. On to the next question, then.

Here it is: Can I actively and diligently pursue a certain uptick in financial resources while honestly saying, "The Lord is my helper; I will not be afraid—what can people do to me?" Lots of layers of nuance here, once again, but the simplest way of checking myself (whether I am *honestly* saying this) is to see whether I can say this regardless of whether my active and diligent pursuit actually nets me any additional income. Does success or failure, in financial terms, dictate whether I say the words of Hebrews 13:6? Do I fall to the accusation Satan levied at Job—that were it not for material success, my faith would fritter away to nothing (Job 1:9-11)?

And one last question: How is God saying, "I will never leave you or forsake you" in my current situation? His voice is hard to hear if all we ever do is try to change our current situation. Faith is recognizing that no step along our journey is something to simply get past. Our natural reaction is to seek the quickest way out of a difficult season. I'm certainly not saying we shouldn't look for a way out. But the lousy job, the financial deficit, the broken relationship, the health crisis—all of these are opportunities to ask, in the midst of the storm, How does God speak to me *in* this situation beyond showing me the way *out* of this situation?[9]

Patience is critical. The normal human response to a season of financial challenges is *get out as fast as you can*. Hebrews, though, invites

---

[9]Just to be clear: it is *not* okay to suggest to a hurting person that the only reason God hasn't brought them out of that hurt is that they haven't yet listened faithfully enough to what God is saying to them in that situation. You don't know that, you can't know that, and saying it is as likely to make things worse as to make them better. God's motivations for taking someone else through a trial are not for you to know.

us to hear God speak in the moment before we pursue solutions to the moment. I need to ask God to remind me how he is keeping me alive in my situation before I ask him to remove me from my situation. If you're tired of hearing me say this, I think that just means you're paying attention: Hebrews is a lot more interested in teaching us to live ectopically than to escape ectopicness.

"The love of money is the root of all evil" (1 Tim 6:10). "You cannot serve God and money" (Mt 6:24). Some things just beg for our worship, and money is right at the top of that list. It isn't really money, of course, but the things that it provides, which means the idol that seduces us isn't money but really ourselves. "The love of *self* is the root of all evil." "You can't serve God and *self*." The antidote to the poison of self-worship, according to Hebrews 13:5-6, is the conversation in which God speaks his word to us, and we speak it back to him, and from that dialogue comes contentment. Not apathy or laziness but contentment that says, "I pursue gain not out of fear but rather out of a desire to give as it has been given to me."

Love and Leaders

Twice in Hebrews 13 we are told to follow our earthly leaders. "Remember your leaders, who spoke the word of God to you; as you consider their life trajectories, imitate their faith" (Heb 13:7). And a bit later: "Be confident in your leaders and submit to them (since they care for you as those who will give an account) so that they can do their jobs with joy instead of complaining, because that wouldn't do you any good" (Heb 13:17).

We'll get to what happens in between these verses in the next section, so hold that thought. First, though, we need to notice how these two verses fit together. Hebrews 13:7 says that it is the task of leaders in the church to *speak God's word to the church*. And Hebrews 13:17 says that those leaders will *give an account*. Both use the term *logos*; in the one to mean "word" and in the other to mean "account." Interestingly enough, the same sort of thing happens in Hebrews 4:12-13, which says, "The word [*logos*] of God is living and active and sharper than any two-edged sword, and it penetrates to the division of soul and spirit and joints and marrow. It discerns the thoughts and intentions of the heart, and no creature is hidden from its sight; all are naked and exposed to the one to whom we must give an account [*logos*]." God's word (*logos*) to us prompts our word (*logos*) to him. It's the same thing that just happened in Hebrews 13:5-6; God speaks to us, and by faith we respond in kind.

We already know we're supposed to imitate Jesus. But let's be honest: Jesus lived a long time ago, in another context, with rather different concerns and challenges and situations. The more you zoom in to your own life, the less it looks like anything Jesus dealt with, and the more difficult it becomes to imitate him within those situations. I have no idea what Jesus would have done in my situation, because he never experienced my situation, or at least the Bible doesn't say that he did. What then? This is one of the great lessons of Hebrews 11, in fact, and it's exactly what's going on here. God puts other people just ahead of us along the same path who have figured out what imitating Jesus looks like to a slightly greater degree than we have. And *those* people have experienced just about exactly the same things I have, and they can encourage me and guide me in what it looks like to imitate Jesus in the most concrete situations of my own life. So when you find those people, pay attention to them. Imitate them. Respect them. Support them. What they're doing right now is what you'll be doing next, and what you're doing right now is what they did last.

Leaders, there's something here for you as well. First, you're hardly the next person in line after Jesus. The whole crowd of witnesses, everyone who went before you, whose faith *you* imitated—don't get caught thinking it's Jesus, then you, then everyone else. Second, you have a very specific job: speak God's word to those whom you lead, and as you do so, keep in mind that you are accountable to the one who sees all, knows all, discerns all.

Leaders, preachers, teachers, pastors, mentors, translators, all those who lead God's people by speaking God's word, in whatever context that may take place—listen carefully to this. God is never absent from his

word. God does not communicate from afar. Where his word is, he is
there also. Look again at Hebrews 4:12-13. When God speaks, he sees all
and knows all, *because he is there*. Do you preach, teach, disciple, and so
on as though God were actually there with you?

Dietrich Bonhoeffer describes the serpent's conversation with Eve
in the Garden of Eden as "the first conversation *about* God, the first
religious, theological conversation."[10] In other words, it's the first time
someone ever talked *about* God rather than *to* God or *with* God—it's
the first time someone spoke of God as though he weren't there. My
systematic theology students and I admonish each other regularly: *do
theology as though God were in the room*. How many times have you
said something about someone that you wouldn't have said if they had
been present? How much more so with God, especially in light of everything Hebrews has said about what it means for God to be present.
Would you talk about a forest fire while standing next to one and
pretend it weren't there?

The last bit of instructions concerning leaders reminds me of what
Paul says in Ephesians 6:4—"Fathers, don't provoke your children!"
The roles are reversed in Hebrews, though. For Paul, the authority
figure ought not to provoke the one under their authority. For Hebrews, those under authority ought not provoke those who exercise
authority over them. Help them do their jobs "with joy and not complaining" (Heb 13:17). You know who you are. Stop thinking your
spiritual gift is criticizing up the chain of command. *Of course* there's
a time and place for constructive criticism, just like in Ephesians
there's a time and a place for fathers to discipline their children. But
as there are fathers (and I've been one at times) who push so hard that
their children are beat down rather than motivated to press on, there
are Christians whose constant negativity destroys their leaders. And
notice how Hebrews concludes the thought in Hebrews 13:17: as the
leader goes, so goes the whole church. A beat-down leader isn't any
good to anybody.

---

[10]Dietrich Bonhoeffer, *Creation and Fall* (Philadelphia: Fortress, 2004), 111.

Love and Life

Enough about leaders. But it's curious, isn't it, how those two statements about leaders are separated by nine verses (Heb 13:8-16) of what-in-the-world-are-you-talking-about? Jesus never changes, so we have a different kind of food from them, because their sacrificial animals get burned outside the camp, so Jesus was outside the camp, so we should go outside the camp, because we're looking for a yet-to-come city, so let's sing praises and be nice to people. That all makes sense, right? As my students and I sometimes ask in class when we come to strange texts: "Is it obvious what that means?" (No.)

Let's start at the beginning. *Jesus never changes* (Heb 13:8). Seems true, seems important, seems entirely disconnected from the surrounding context. But it isn't. Notice the three contrasts: sustenance (Heb 13:9-10), sacrifices (Heb 13:11-12, 15-16), and residences (Heb 13:13-14).

First contrast: sustenance. How does God keep us alive in our ectopic state? *God speaks.* We have a spiritual food source (i.e., teaching) that is neither foreign nor constantly shifting, because our leaders speak God's word in Christ, and that never changes because Christ never changes.

Let me say that again: God's word in Christ never changes, because Christ never changes. Many of us in the church need to pay more careful attention to the frequent admonition that we not be the kind of people who jump from bandwagon to bandwagon without any sense of the defining center (see Eph 4:14 and Jas 1:6, for example). The defining center is Christ. People will always be coming along with new fantastic ideas about how to lock in your spiritual health or the health of your church. Those ideas will never actually be new, and they'll usually have some merit in them. Seeker sensitivity. Spiritual disciplines. Nine Marks. Missional living. Whatever. All true and biblical and helpful to a point, and none the actual, unchanging center. That seat belongs to Christ and Christ alone.

On the other hand, and this needs to be said so we don't take the previous point in the wrong way: contextualization is a thing. Communicate in a way that actually communicates. If I speak English to people who don't speak English, I haven't said anything. And you can apply that all the way down: gender, ethnicity, economics, personal history, and so on. The more I know about my audience, the more I tailor my words to fit that audience, the more effective my communication will be. The constancy of God's word in Christ is not a license to preach the same message in the same way over and over and over regardless of the audience or the circumstances, and then complain because "no one wants to listen to truth anymore."

Second contrast: sacrifices. The metaphors are going to get mixed here, so watch carefully. The food that sustains us is likened to the sacrificial leftovers that are eaten by the Levitical priests (Lev 6:16-18, for example), and since the sacrifice of Christ that sustains us happens beyond the orbit of the Levitical cult, those priests have no right to participate in the meal. Not their ritual → not their leftovers. Not only that, but Jesus was crucified "outside the camp," just like the sacrificial leftovers that the priests were *not* to eat were taken outside the camp and burned. To be thrown outside the camp was to be declared unfit for priestly sustenance and of no further use for the work of atonement. Ergo, the sacrificial work that feeds us offers no sustenance to them, and vice versa.

It's not explicit that the Lord's Supper/Communion/Eucharist is in view here, but it would make a lot of sense if it was. We are kept alive by the food that Christ provides for us in his sacrifice. What else would that be? He offers us a feast. You might be familiar with C. S. Lewis's *The Last Battle*—if so, recall the scene toward the end where the dwarves are in the world through the stable, and a fantastic feast has been set before them, and they refuse to eat. Likewise we, if we refuse the bread and the cup.[11]

Third contrast: residences (and then back to sacrifices once more). "Outside the camp" is now symbolic not of cultic leftovers but of social rejection. Jesus "bore reproach," some versions say, when he suffered outside the camp (Heb 13:13), and we are encouraged to follow him there

---

[11]I am aware that there are churches that do not practice Communion, and I grieve for them.

and do likewise. In fact, the first recipients of this sermon have already been doing this: they had in the not-so-distant past endured suffering, trouble, *reproach*, imprisonment, and property theft (Heb 10:32-35). Hebrews also tells us that Moses "considered the *reproach* that comes on those who follow the Messiah to be greater than all of Egypt's treasures" (Heb 11:26). Now notice the pattern in every case: Moses "was looking ahead to his reward" (Heb 11:26). The readers of Hebrews "knew that they had a better and lasting possession," which they would receive in due time (Heb 10:34-36). Jesus himself "despised the shame of the cross" in anticipation of the glory he would receive when he sat down at his Father's right hand (Heb 12:2). And now we too "have no lasting city here but are seeking the city which is still to come" (Heb 13:14).

So the good news, in the great missionary Jim Elliot's classic phrase: he is no fool who gives what he cannot keep to gain what he cannot lose. But there's another side to that coin: Jesus' journey outside the camp precedes his ascension and exaltation and rule over God's creation, and so must ours. Before the crown comes the cross. It's one of the most common exhortations in all of the New Testament and one of the most difficult: we must die with Christ in order to be raised with him. To live while out of place so as to someday come into place doesn't just mean following Jesus into his kingdom, into his glory—it means taking the same route he took to get there.

That route is generally described positively in Hebrews: "entering in" (Heb 4:1, 10; 9:24-25) or "approaching"/"drawing near" (Heb 4:16; 7:25; 12:22).[12] But here it is described negatively: "going out" (Heb 13:13). You have to leave one space to enter another. And look: we are supposed to

---

[12]There's a debate among scholars as to whether "drawing near" and "entering in" describe two different actions in Hebrews. For affirmation of that distinction, see Nicholas J. Moore, "'In' or 'Near'? Heavenly Access and Christian Identity in Hebrews," in *Muted Voices of the New Testament: Readings in the Catholic Epistles and Hebrews*, ed. Katherine Hockey, Madison N. Pierce, and Francis Watson, Library of New Testament Studies 587 (London: T&T Clark, 2017), 185-98. And for rejection of the distinction, see Scott D. Mackie, "'Let Us Draw Near . . . but Not Too Near': A Critique of the Attempted Distinction Between 'Drawing Near' and 'Entering' in Hebrews' Entry Exhortations," in *Listen, Understand, Obey: Essays on Hebrews in Honor of Gareth T. Cockerill*, ed. Caleb T. Friedeman (Eugene, OR: Pickwick, 2017), 17-36.

exit *now*, and yet we won't fully enter for quite some time. So where are we now? What one scholar calls a "permanent liminality."[13] A liminal space is a space-in-between, a no-man's-land, an un-locatedness that comes with being neither here nor there, in the "already-not-yet," as New Testament scholars often call our chronological location between Jesus already inaugurating his kingdom but not yet fully establishing it.

This is how we stay alive. We are already in the unshakable kingdom because we are in Jesus. Think back to chapter nine: that mystery we call "union with Christ." It means we are where he is, and since he is in heaven, we're there with him. And we act out being with him there by going where he went here. He, Jesus, who is life himself, entered into a lifeless world; he went outside the camp, ostracized and cut off from the lifelines of his people. So we go there too. We stop seeking life where it can't be found anyway and instead follow our faithful high priest, who keeps us alive now and leads us to life later.

Now, back to sacrifices for a moment. It might seem like the most obvious thing in the world, on Hebrews' terms, that those who receive their life from Jesus do not need to offer sacrifices. Atonement is complete, there is one great high priest, and that's all there is to say about that. And yet here we find, in Hebrews 13:15-16, three sacrifices that we are still to offer: a sacrifice of *praise*, a sacrifice of *good works*, and a sacrifice of *sharing* (or *generosity*). These three things seem like rather generically Christian things to do, so we ought to pause and meditate a bit not on why they are commanded (which is hopefully obvious) but on why they are *sacrifices*.

First, the sacrifice of *praise* is reminiscent of Jesus' words to the Father, spoken in the midst of his suffering outside the camp: "I will declare your name to my siblings; in the midst of the assembly I will praise you!" (Heb 2:12). Jesus is quoting Psalm 22 (the one the Gospels use so frequently to tell the story of Jesus' crucifixion), and these words are spoken by the unnamed righteous sufferer in that moment when, despite the

---

[13]David A. DeSilva, *Perseverance in Gratitude: A Socio-rhetorical Commentary on the Epistle "to the Hebrews"* (Grand Rapids, MI: Eerdmans, 2000), 503.

fact that nothing has changed circumstantially, he declares his belief that God will rescue him and he will once again have the opportunity to praise his rescuer. These are the sorts of things we say when we have been brought through death into resurrection life.

Second, sacrifices of praise ("praise sacrifices") are not an invention of the author of Hebrews. They've been around as long as atoning sacrifices, actually, described in Leviticus 7:12-16 as an offering that said, "Thanks!" to God after the atoning offering was complete. "Thanks for accepting that life in place of mine!" So when we come to God, we don't go atoning-offering-then-praise-offering; we just start praising, because the atoning-offering part of the equation is already taken care of. There's also precedent in the Psalms for praise sacrifices that didn't involve any offering at all—the praise was itself the sacrifice (Ps 50:14; 107:22). That's what Hebrews commands: our "sacrifice" is the "fruit of lips that confess his name" (Heb 13:15).

Third, though such actions were seldom called sacrifices prior to this point, the idea that God is more impressed with love for our neighbors than with our animal offerings is all over the place in the Bible.[14] This is why we "do not neglect" hospitality (Heb 13:2) and we "do not neglect" doing good and sharing generously with others (Heb 13:16). And don't forget: all this is framed as *worship* that is pleasing to God (Heb 12:28-29).

Here's the most important thing: it's worship in response to atonement, not worship in pursuit of or anticipation of atonement. It's not that our generosity and good deeds are the new atoning offering (as though it used to be animals and their blood, but now it's random acts of kindness).[15] Love of one's neighbor is a form of praise offering, not atoning offering. We give because we have received; we do not give so that we may receive. Ever been generous out of guilt? With such sacrifices God is *not* pleased.

Once Israel was judged because its people thought they could buy their way out of sin when the value of their currency had dropped due

---

[14]One other ancient Jewish writer does say that "the one who gives alms offers a sacrifice of praise" (Sirach 35:2), and Paul calls the financial gifts he received from the Philippian church "an acceptable sacrifice" (Phil 4:18).

[15]Koester, *Hebrews*, 578.

to their flagrant injustice. Now we are judged if we think we can buy our way out of sin when no such currency exists other than the blood of Jesus, and the transaction has already been completed. The atoning angle on sacrifice is complete: "Where there is forgiveness, there no longer remains any further offering for sins" (Heb 10:18). But Hebrews agrees wholeheartedly with the Old Testament that when you walk into God's presence and receive atonement there, your next move is to say, "Thanks," and then get back out there and pass God's fantastic generosity on to others. We are conduits of life, not just recipients of it.

So here we are, at Hebrews 13:17, back to "Obey your leaders." And that raises the final question of this part: Why do two commands about the people in charge of the church bracket a paragraph about food and altars and sacrifices? There's potentially a contrast between past leaders (Heb 13:7) and present leaders (Heb 13:17), held together by the same Jesus Christ, head over both. There's also a sense of leaders ahead of us, calling us forward (Heb 13:7), and leaders behind us, spurring us on (Heb 13:17). Beyond those connections, I see two things worthy of our attention.

First, being alive in Jesus includes being part of a group of other people who are likewise alive in Jesus. "Union with Christ means union with others who are in him too."[16] Speaking practically, we won't, or maybe *can't*, go outside the camp after Jesus without being supported and led by others who are doing the same but have a bit more wisdom or experience than we do. This is why, earlier, Hebrews connects ignoring our Christian community as a waypoint on the road to apostasy (Heb 10:25). Reject the people of God, and eventually we'll reject God himself. If that doesn't scare you, go back and read Deuteronomy again.

Second, the middle section about sustenance and sacrifices and residences tells us what to look for, what exactly we ought to imitate and obey in our leaders. If they aren't feeding us properly (strengthening us by grace, focusing us on Christ, inviting us to the table), if they aren't worshiping with reverent awe through praise and generosity, if they

---

[16]Kevin J. Vanhoozer, *Biblical Interpretation After Babel* (Grand Rapids, MI: Brazos, 2016), 150-51.

aren't imitating Jesus by taking on the stigma of rejecting the eternality of earthly kingdoms and systems and rewards and values, we've got the wrong leaders.

Study Questions

1. Have you ever thought about what God was doing before he created us? Does it matter?

2. How do you see your cultural context (whether in the church or outside it) bent toward treating sex as "common"? How are you tempted to follow suit?

3. Do you struggle with financial contentment? How do you wrestle with the tension between legitimate desire for a wider stewardship and trusting that God really can take care of you?

4. Are you a leader who speaks God's words? How have you ensured that you listen (to God) before you speak (to others)?

5. Are you tempted to be a thorn in the flesh of your leaders? How can you support them and encourage them instead?

6. Are you giving God the sacrifices of praise, good works, and generosity? Which of these is the hardest for you?

17

FEELING OUT OF PLACE?

IN JUNE 2018, MY JOB WENT AWAY. Well, the announcement happened on November 8, 2017. There were rumblings, but since I was the youngest and cheapest professor on the faculty, since nearly all of my classes were in the general education core (Bible classes at a Bible college), and since we had plenty of students and plenty of resources to weather some storms, I wasn't too worried. Teaching the gen-ed core meant job stability—I had joked that they'd have to turn the lights off altogether to get rid of me. Joke's on me. They turned the lights off. It wasn't just my job that went away. It was the whole school.

Fast-forward eight hours. That very evening, just hours after the announcement, one of our professors went home and googled "how to start a new university in the state of Washington." We google things we don't know anything about, right? A few hallway conversations, a few casual hints, and within days there were evening meetings happening at one of our houses.

I wasn't there for the first couple of meetings, because I'd been offered a lifeline—a faculty appointment at another school. Here I was, stuck in Spokane. We'd just bought our first house, we had three little ones, the job market in my field (university faculty posts in biblical studies) was horrible. I felt, well, I felt ectopic. Like there was no life for me there. And then I got an invitation to get out.

I'm a missionary kid. Before Spokane I had lived in Maine, Connecticut, Ohio, Texas, Illinois, California (northern and southern), and Thailand.

And I've always had a pretty easy time packing up and moving on. It's been real, it's been fun, I'm ready for the next thing. By faith Abraham *went*—I'm down for that cause. But this time was different. I wasn't ready to leave Spokane. People I respect told me, "You *have* to take that other job. If you spend a year out of the academic space, if there's a gap in your resume, you're done. You'll never get hired again." But I couldn't do it. I wasn't ready to go. By faith Abraham *stayed*—that was a new one for me. But we stayed, because we sensed that's what God wanted us to do.

Back to those evening meetings. I think I missed the first three or four, and then I, joining a group of my friends and colleagues, decided to take a leap of faith. We spent the next few months creating bylaws, curriculum, catalogs, policies and procedures; we fundraised, we recruited board members, we did all the things that needed to be done. We submitted our application to the state of Washington in March, and then we waited. And waited. And waited. And on August 20, 2018, we received our license to be a degree-granting institution. Great Northern University.

We stayed in Spokane. How was I going to support my family there? How was I going to advance my career there? I was ectopic. I'm still ectopic. August 20, 2018, didn't change that. So we have a school now. That's amazing and incredible and miraculous, but it doesn't mean we've landed that leap of faith. That was the beginning of the real work, not the end of it. We still haven't come to the end of it. We still walk by faith.

I tell this story, eight years later, because I think my journey with Great Northern University illustrates particularly well the connection between the life of faith in Hebrews 11, the life of love in Hebrews 13, and the need to receive life from God in the midst of our journeys. Notice I didn't say it illustrates my successful navigation of those things. The past eight years have been difficult in many ways, not the least of which has been financial. As any entrepreneur will tell you, when you start something you get paid if there's money, and you don't if there isn't. And so we walk by faith, on the one hand, and we fight *constantly* against the (unrequited) love of money, on the other.

We can't love money and walk by faith, because to love money means to pursue it as a means to an improper end, and that end is happiness.

Meaning. Fulfillment. Contentment. Satisfaction. Life. To walk by faith is to acknowledge our dying condition and rely on the God who raises the dead. To love money is to grasp vainly at immortality, to seek life where it may not be found. Great Northern University remains *alive* today not ultimately because it has succeeded in finding students, donors, and so on, but because it has believed and will continue to believe in the God who brings beauty from ashes and life from death.

My own personal well-being will proceed in similar fashion. I have no guarantee that I will ever find the kind of financial security that (I am tempted to believe) puts me beyond the need for faith, and I have every guarantee that orbiting my life around that pursuit will end in failure and misery. And, contrasted with that, I have the strongest possible guarantee that, as the hymn puts it, "One with himself [Christ], I cannot die."[1] I cannot die. His indestructible life is *mine*. Love of money, love of pleasure, seeking life and meaning from professional success—for the one who is in Christ, this is like putting a plastic tarp on a tank to protect it from a .22 pistol. The tarp won't help, and the tank didn't need it anyways. Christ keeps us alive, and we walk by faith in him, not in our ability to construct a veneer of self-fulfillment.

The life of faith is not at odds with the life of wisdom, financial or otherwise. Faith in Hebrews 11 and generosity in Hebrews 13 are not invitations to haphazard spending, senseless giving, or other kinds of financial foolishness. My fellow entrepreneurs and I at Great Northern University meet regularly to talk about how to get *out* of our current situation—how to increase enrollment, fundraising, and so forth. We don't want to live on the knife's edge of viability. We don't want to know that losing a couple of students next semester could mean a pay cut. But that's where we are, and we are there for both natural reasons (we're a startup in a market that is, broadly speaking, both overcrowded in terms of competition and shrinking in terms of demand) and supernatural reasons (God has something for us to learn in *this* season, regardless of how long it takes to get to the next season). Ultimately, the lesson we are

---

[1] "Before the Throne of God Above," lyrics by Charitie Lees Bancroft, music by Vikki Cook.

trying to learn is that we walk by faith, not by fundraising, and our lives are secured by divine power, not enrollment or endowment.

Over the past eight years, we've developed a few specific practices (some at the office, some in the home) that have helped us walk by faith rather than by finance, so to speak. We start every academic year by reminding each other that God's guarantee of success belongs to the church as a whole, not to our school. "Faith in the promises of God" doesn't mean believing that Great Northern University will become what we want it to become. It's a reality check; we're naming what's been guaranteed and what hasn't. To believe God will do something that he hasn't actually promised to do is dangerous, so we go out of our way to remind each other that God's triumph over evil is inevitable, but the participation of Great Northern University in that triumph is not.

Immediately after acknowledging the tenuousness of our situation, we tell stories of how God has kept Great Northern University alive in the preceding academic years. Stories about students, stories about faculty and staff, stories about accreditation, and, of course, stories about money. Back in 2018, when there were no paychecks because there was no money, Annie and I started a list, on yellow legal paper, of various financial provisions. A paid preaching gig, a tax return, a friend paying for our plane tickets so we could see family for the holidays; the list went on, and on, and—that list is five or six pages long at this point and still growing. I'm going to keep adding to that list until the day that I die, and I'm going to keep showing it to my team at Great Northern University until the day that I retire, because that list says, "Let love of money have no place in you." It says, "If God is for us, who can be against us?" It says, "Your life is hidden with Christ in God."

Part of walking by faith is staying on mission. Higher education, like any business, is full of shiny objects. "Hey, that product is selling for them; we should sell that product too!" Here's how that works in colleges and universities. We notice that a certain academic program is popular. We have enrollment problems, so we're looking for academic programs that attract students. Problem, solution, boom. Done. Right? No. Not even close. For one thing, it takes years (not to mention millions of

dollars) to get new academic programs up and running; by the time
yours is ready to go, the market has moved on, and that program isn't
popular anymore. Oops. More importantly, though, is the fact that "Can
product x make us money?" is the wrong question, or at least the wrong
first question. The right *first* question is, "Does product x accomplish
our mission?" Staying on mission requires walking by faith, because it
isn't distracted by trying to solve the wrong problem even when that
wrong problem is the one staring everyone in the face.

Remember when Jesus said, "Seek first God's kingdom, and everything else you're constantly worried about will be taken care of" (Mt 6:33)?
I don't think he meant, "Spend every waking moment telling people
about me, and food and shelter and clothing will magically appear on
your doorstep." Not that he couldn't pull that off if he wanted to. But I
think he meant something more like, "Stay on mission, stay on course,
walk by faith, and see how I take care of your legitimate daily needs." And
the ways that he might do that are practically limitless: gifts, deals, raises,
opportunities—all these are ways that everything I'm constantly worried
about will be taken care of. But when Great Northern University says,
"We're not going to start that program because it doesn't fit our mission,
even though it looks like it might make us money," what we're really
saying is, "We have *this* job to do, *this* problem to solve. And we trust that
if we stay faithful to *this* mission, God—insofar as he wants us to continue that mission—will find ways to keep us alive on that path."

Study Questions

1. What unnecessary and unhelpful safeguards are you tempted to
   put in place—things that might make you feel better about your
   situation, but don't actually help?

2. Do you consistently and intentionally tell stories of God's faithfulness in your community (family, local church, business, etc.)?
   If not, how could you begin doing that?

3. Are you tempted to avoid difficulties by always jumping ship and
   trying something new? How can you stay on mission, by faith,
   and persevere through those difficulties?

CONCLUSION

WE LIVE IN A LIFELESS WORLD. What does that mean? What does it mean to *live*? We are creatures. That means we were created by someone else, and we were created for reasons determined in advance by that someone else. *Life* means being what we were created to be, doing what we were created to do. And that means (among other things) healthy, full, mutually beneficial relationships in every direction: with each other, with ourselves, with the nonhuman portions of God's creation, and with God himself. And that is precisely what we don't have, what we *can't* have, in our current location in its current state. We are broken and disintegrated, and everything else in all creation is broken and disintegrated, and I can't have a relationship with something else if I am not one integrated thing in the first place. So I am dying. I am alone. I am afraid. I am discontent. I am fragmented. And yet. And yet I live.

How is that life possible? We are in the world, but we are also in Christ. In him, our resurrected and enthroned high priest, we are kept alive as long as the world remains under the dominion of sin, until he brings heaven to earth and makes all things new. He is the source of that life-from-without. How is that life appropriated? By faith. Faith that stays, faith that goes, faith that sees, faith that submits to the call of God to remain close to him in every circumstance. How is that life manifested? By love. Love for those like us, love for those unlike us, love for all that is good and right and sacred in the world.

Hebrews starts in the middle: the ascension of Jesus. The ascension is *the* pivotal event in all of history if the question at hand is, How am I alive when death is all around me? I am alive because at the ascension, the Father welcomed his Son ("sit at my right hand" [Heb 1:13]), and the

Son introduced me to the Father ("Here I am, along with the children you gave me" [Heb 2:13]). Of course, before he ascended he descended—to the earth, to the grave. He took on my death even while never completely relinquishing hold of his life, and now death has no more permanent claim on me than it has on him.

Onward and upward he went—up from the grave, up from the earth. Up into the highest heaven, a human being, the most human human, we might say, because he alone can do and is doing what we were created to do. He presented himself in heaven as the body and blood of the new covenant, he cleansed the very space in which his Father and I can now meet and do business, he took his place as the one who never stops reminding me that I am his, I am loved, I am alive.

We are designed to be conduits, not repositories. Life flowing into us from Christ is meant to keep moving from us into others. Otherwise it stagnates. Otherwise it stinks. That new covenant is not just an invitation to *have* life; it is an invitation to *live*—to live in relation to others and in relation to the world around us. Covenants come with expectations. When Israel failed to live up to those expectations, when they did not keep their side of the bargain, God kept his. As then, so now. God will never fail to sustain until the end those who walk by faith and live in love, nor will he fail to judge those who refuse to do so.

Hebrews is a difficult book—difficult to understand and much more difficult to obey—and yet it is powerful in the midst of that difficulty. If we're paying close attention, it should frighten us a little bit (or a lot). It should get under our skin. It should provide plenty of food for thought, and not all that food will taste good. If you've really let Hebrews take hold of you in the process of reading this book, there's some turmoil in your soul. I think that's a good thing. I think the author of Hebrews knew that would happen. And I think that's why he begins his ending by calling God a God of *peace*.

> Now may the God of peace, the one who through the blood of an eternal covenant raised Jesus, the great Shepherd of the sheep, up from the dead—may *that God* equip you with every good thing

that you need to do his will, and may he accomplish in us, through Jesus Christ, what pleases him, and may Jesus receive glory forever and ever. Amen. (Heb 13:20-21)

Hebrews offers two truths side by side, and for many of us the harder truth is the one that needs to take hold first. *Seek life where it may be found—by dying to yourself and walking by faith in Jesus. Endure the cross and despise its shame. Enter the presence of a holy and awesome and overwhelming God whose fire consumes his enemies.* These are not instructions to be taken lightly, and it is a good thing if we tremble a bit as we consider the inadequacy of our obedience to them thus far.

The intensity of Hebrews, the warnings, the fire and curses and apostasy and rejection—these are only half the story. The other half is that our faithful pioneer and brother and high priest, Jesus, does not merely run ahead of us and expect us to keep up. He walks alongside us every step of the way. He gives leaders whose example we can follow as they nourish us with God's grace. He speaks the truths of God's Word to us. When we follow him into the presence of his Father, the door is wide open, no longer barred by veils or cherubim or anything else, and we are welcomed in.

We are not God's adversaries who cringe in terror, who "shrink back to destruction," as Hebrews 10:39 puts it. We are the Son's siblings (Heb 2:12), we are God's children (Heb 2:13), we are those to whom the unbreakable oath has been spoken: "I will never leave you or forsake you" (Heb 13:5). *Peace.* "We have a high priest who is seated at the right hand of God in heaven" (Heb 8:1). *Peace.* "Because he suffered when he was tempted, he is able to help those who are being tempted" (Heb 2:18). *Peace.* "He destroyed the one who has the power of death—the devil—and delivered us from being enslaved to the fear of death" (Heb 2:14-15). *Peace.* "I am confident of better things for you, beloved—things that go with salvation" (Heb 6:9). *Peace.*

Not long ago, I had one of those nights where, when I woke up in the morning, all seventeen unrelated dreams I'd just had were as vivid as if I were still experiencing every one of them, and a couple of them were maybe the most intense dreams I've ever had. My conversation with God that morning went like this:

Me: I'm pretty fried right now.

God: Peace.

Me: What kind of peace?

God: My peace.

Me: I don't know what that means.

God: What troubles you?

Me: Everything, apparently.

God: Peace.

Me: How?

God: I have overcome the world.

Me: What stresses of mine are clouding my vision to that fact?

God: All of them.

Me: Well, obviously. Where do I start?

God: Start by not acting like you have to overcome the world. I already did that, remember?

I have overcome the world. This world is killing us, and we are killing it. Like a baby desperately scrapping for every molecule of nutrition it can get from a mother's fallopian tube, we are trying to overcome our ectopicness. And in the process, we drain what little life there is around us while never coming close to finding enough to sustain us. We are trying to overcome the reality of the world. It's not going to work. In this world we will have trouble. In this world we will be out of place. But he has overcome the world, he has overcome Death itself. He keeps us alive and will keep us alive in Christ until the end. *Peace.*

When I lose something I thought I couldn't live without. *Peace.*

When I feel the walls closing in financially. *Peace.*

When I can't maintain the pace and can't see to the next Sabbath. *Peace.*

When I can't seem to do anything right. *Peace.*

When my home is in chaos. *Peace.*

When nothing goes according to my plan. Or I don't have a plan. Or someone rejected my plan. *Peace.*

How does he do this? How does God speak *peace* into our hearts, a peace not based on wishful thinking but on his ability to do what he has promised? Back to the text: *he raised Jesus Christ from the dead* (Heb 13:20). Given that the "raising" language here is not the typical language used to describe the resurrection event, and given Hebrews' interest in not only the resurrection but in the events that follow it (ascension and atonement and enthronement), this phrase here may have that whole sequence in view.[1] He didn't just resuscitate Jesus. He didn't just put the breath of life back in him. He raised him up from the ground, up from the earth, up above the angels, up above *everything*. And that's what he's doing with us too. He is raising us by "equipping us with every good thing that we need to do his will," and "accomplishing in us, through Jesus Christ, what pleases him" (Heb 13:21). All that God asks of you, he makes possible, and all that God requires of you, he makes actual. God is no sideline reporter, waiting to officially record your success or failure, whichever it may happen to be. He has some skin in this game, you might say—he is personally invested in your success, and he's not willing to stand idly by and hope against hope that you get the job done.

There's no single analogy that does God justice. He's the coach who trains us, the teammate who encourages us, the fan who cheers us, the judge who evaluates us, the breath in our lungs, the fuel in our system. There is no element of our performance that is not powered by the God who has done and continues to do all that is necessary to keep us coming. He does all this through his Son, Jesus Christ. His Son the priest, his Son

---

[1]Hebrews 13:20 uses *anagō*, while *egeirō* is the more common term. Some scholars have suggested that the resurrection is *not* in view here, but that suggestion has not held up to close scrutiny. See, helpfully, David M. Moffitt, *Atonement and the Logic of the Resurrection in the Epistle to the Hebrews*, Supplements to Novum Testamentum 141 (Leiden: Brill, 2011), 24-28; R. B. Jamieson, *Jesus' Death and Heavenly Offering in Hebrews*, Society for New Testament Studies Monograph Series 172 (Cambridge: Cambridge University Press, 2019), 156-59.

the sacrifice, his Son the pioneer. And it is fitting that we end here, as Hebrews does, by setting our gaze squarely on the one who both lives and keeps us alive and by offering our sacrifice of praise to him. To him be glory, forever and ever, Amen.

— Going Deeper —

THE OLD TESTAMENT
IN HEBREWS

Exposition/Exhortation and the Structure of Hebrews

Every book of the Bible, in its own way, contains both "what is true" and "what to do." Both the *is* and the *ought*, the indicative and the imperative, the orthodoxy and the orthopraxy. So, for example, in Ephesians 1–3 there's a whole lot of truth about what God has done for us in Christ. And then in Ephesians 4–6, there's a whole lot of practical reflection on how we should conduct ourselves in the world, given that we are in fact in Christ.

What's somewhat unique about Hebrews is how the "what is true" is so thoroughly grounded in the Old Testament—to the point that scholars in fact call the two threads of Hebrews exposition and exhortation. Meaning that Hebrews has two things going on: exposition/explanation of the Old Testament, and exhortation to the audience to live in light of that explanation. And it's not like Ephesians, where the first half of the book is explanation and the second half is exhortation. Instead, it's a constant flow back and forth: Explain Psalm 8, exhort to life based on Psalm 8. Explain Psalm 95, exhort to life based on Psalm 95. Explain Psalm 110, exhort to life based on Psalm 110. From one to the other, back and forth, the whole way through the book. The point being, of course, that the use of the Old Testament in Hebrews and the structure of the book of Hebrews are inextricable from each other.

Further Resources

Guthrie, George H. *The Structure of Hebrews: A Text-Linguistic Analysis*. Biblical Studies Library. Grand Rapids, MI: Baker, 1998.

Joslin, Barry C. "Can Hebrews Be Structured? An Assessment of Eight Approaches." *Currents in Biblical Research* 6 (2007): 99-129.

Martin, Michael W., and Jason A. Whitlark. *Inventing Hebrews: Design and Purpose in Ancient Rhetoric.* Society for New Testament Studies Monograph Series 171. Cambridge: Cambridge University Press, 2018.

Westfall, Cynthia L. *A Discourse Analysis of the Letter to the Hebrews: The Relationship Between Form and Meaning.* Library of New Testament Studies 297. London: T&T Clark, 2005.

Citations, Allusions, and Echoes

Scholars often use three terms to distinguish uses of the Old Testament in the New Testament. A *citation* is a direct quote, like when Matthew 1:22 says, "All this happened to fulfill what was spoken by the prophet," and then quotes exactly the words of Isaiah 7:14, "The virgin will conceive and give birth to a son, and they will call him Immanuel." An *allusion* happens when it's fairly clear that a New Testament author has a particular text in mind, but the wording isn't exactly the same, like when Jesus takes three guys up a mountain, his face gets really bright, Moses is there, and God speaks out of a cloud. The Gospel writers don't have to quote part of the Sinai narratives—if you've ever read the book of Exodus, it's impossible to read the transfiguration and *not* think about Mount Sinai. And an *echo* is a subtler version of an allusion, like when you are reading your Bible and something on the page in front of you reminds you of something you read somewhere else in the Bible. So you read about Jesus being in Gethsemane, and a young man runs away and leaves his clothes behind—and that reminds you of another time when something similar happened, way back when Joseph was fleeing Potiphar's wife. It's not obvious what the point of that connection is, and it's not even obvious that the Gospel of Mark made that connection on purpose. It's just a little something that makes you stop and say, "Huh—I wonder whether there's something there?"

Hebrews, of course, has many citations (Ps 2; 8; 95; 110; Deut 32; Jer 31 being prominent among them). It also has lots of clear allusions: to the Day of Atonement (Lev 16), to the encounter between Melchizedek and Abraham (Gen 14), to Israel's encounter with God at Mount Sinai (Ex 19–20), and, of course, to all kinds of Old Testament stories in its retelling of the biblical story in Hebrews 11. But identifying echoes in Hebrews is a little tougher, because the Old Testament references tend to be so clearly identified; one plausible candidate would be the reference to Christ "bearing the sins of many" in Hebrews 9:28, which sounds like what the Suffering Servant will do according to Isaiah 53:12. The context in Hebrews is about the Day of Atonement in relation to Christ's heavenly work and in anticipation of final judgment, so it isn't obvious that the author of Hebrews has Isaiah 53 in mind. But that one phrase is unique enough to these two texts that it's at least worth exploring.

Further Resources

Barth, Markus. "Old Testament in Hebrews: An Essay in Biblical Hermeneutics." In *Current Issues in New Testament Interpretation*, edited by William Klassen and Graydon F. Snyder, 53-78. New York: Harper, 1962.

Docherty, Susan. *The Use of the Old Testament in Hebrews: A Case Study in Early Jewish Bible Interpretation*. Wissenschaftliche Untersuchungen zum Neuen Testament 2/260. Tübingen: Mohr Siebeck, 2009.

Dyer, Bryan R. "The Epistle to the Hebrews in Recent Research: Studies on the Author's Identity, His Use of the Old Testament, and Theology." *Journal of Greco-Roman Christianity and Judaism* 9 (2013): 104-31.

Guthrie, George H. "Hebrews." In *Commentary on the New Testament Use of the Old Testament*, edited by Gregory K. Beale and Donald A. Carson, 919-95. Grand Rapids, MI: Baker Academic, 2007.

———. "Hebrews' Use of the Old Testament: Recent Trends in Research." *Currents in Biblical Research* 1 (2003): 271-94.

Hays, Richard B. *Echoes of Scripture in the Letters of Paul*. New Haven, CT: Yale University Press, 1993.

Steyn, Gert J. *A Quest for the Assumed LXX Vorlage of the Explicit Quotations in Hebrews*. Forschungen zur Religion und Literatur des Alten und Neuen Testaments 235. Göttingen: Vandenhoeck & Ruprecht, 2011.

Prosopology

One relative newcomer to the extensive scholarly conversation about Hebrews and the Old Testament is something called prosopological exegesis. It's a modern term for an ancient practice, and it alludes to the *prosōpon*, the "faces" or "characters," that would be exchanged by actors at various points in a theatrical production. If I were to play the part of Ebeneezer Scrooge in the Christmas story, I'd put on the persona, the character, of Scrooge while I was on stage.

There are times in the New Testament where Jesus appears to take on a persona, or a character, from an Old Testament text. The classic example is when, in Acts 2:25-32 (citing Ps 16:8-11), Peter says, "I know David said 'God, you won't let me stay dead,' but David is still dead. So the real performer of that script can't be David—it's actually Jesus!" It's as though the New Testament writers read their Scriptures, the Old Testament, as a script for a screenplay, and Jesus was delivering the ultimate performance of that screenplay. Jesus has put on the *prosōpon* supplied by David in that psalm.

There are many examples of this sort of thing in Hebrews. Right at the very beginning, for example, we find Psalm 2:7. Psalm 2 was scripted as a celebration of the enthronement of the Davidic king—and, according to Hebrews 1:5, the ultimate enthronement of the Davidic king happened at Jesus' ascension. Psalm 22 was scripted by David in his experience of unjust suffering—and, according to Hebrews 2:12, the pinnacle of unjust suffering (and righteous lament within that suffering) took place when Jesus died on the cross.

Further Resources

Bates, Matthew W. *The Birth of the Trinity: Jesus, God, and Spirit in New Testament and Early Christian Interpretations of the Old Testament*. Oxford: Oxford University Press, 2015.

———. *The Hermeneutics of the Apostolic Proclamation*. Waco, TX: Baylor University Press, 2012.

Dyer, Bryan R. "'In the Midst of the Assembly I Will Praise You': Hebrews 2.12 and Its Contribution to the Argument of the Epistle." *Journal for the Study of the New Testament* 43 (2021): 523-38.

Pierce, Madison N. *Divine Discourse in the Epistle to the Hebrews*. Society for New Testament Studies Monograph Series 178. Cambridge: Cambridge University Press, 2020.

CHRISTOLOGY

THE CHALCEDONIAN DEFINITION (AD 451) says that Jesus is "truly God and truly man," being "one person" but having "two natures." To say that Jesus is one person is to say that Jesus is one acting subject—whatever he does, *he* does. It's not the God part of him doing one thing and the human part of him doing another. It also means, though, that he is simultaneously everything one must be in order to be God and everything one must be in order to be human. That's what it means for him to have two natures.

Here's how that plays out in real time. First, when the Son of God took on flesh (the incarnation), he didn't stop being God. At all. Not even a little bit. Prior to the incarnation, he was one (divine) person, with one (divine) nature. After the incarnation, he was one (divine) person with two (divine and human) natures. So the only thing that changed was that he added to himself all that was required of someone to fit into the category human. Paul describes this as a sort of subtraction by addition in Philippians 2:6, where Jesus "emptied himself by taking on the form of a servant"—meaning that the emptying was not a putting off of something divine but a taking on of something human. So as he walks around the streets of Galilee, as he falls asleep on a boat, as he dies on a cross, he's fully and completely God.

Second, when the Son of God took on flesh, he entered into something from which he has never and will never depart. He became human and has been that way ever since. When you see him seated at the right hand of the throne of God in heaven, you're looking at a *man*. A resurrected and glorified man, to be sure, but still a man.

Third, everything Jesus experienced from conception onward, he experienced as both man and God. This is why Chalcedon insists that we call Mary the "Mother of God"—not the mother of the human nature of Jesus, or the mother of the human part of Jesus, or something like that. *God* experienced human birth. He also experienced human death. The God of the Bible can't die, you might think—that doesn't make any sense! True. But God can experience the human experience of dying. What's it like to die? I don't know, personally. But Jesus, the divine Son of God, does.

Jesus also knows what it's like to rise from the dead. This is a bit tricky, but Christian theologians have affirmed a couple of things throughout the centuries. First, that Christ *was raised* from the dead because of his humanity, and that Christ *rose* from the dead because of his deity. Second, that because there is only one God, every action of that one God is a simultaneous act of Father, Son, and Spirit—this doctrine is called *inseparable operations*. In the case of the resurrection, the biblical witness most often ascribes agency to the Father, but also on occasion to the Spirit and even to the Son himself. Who raised Jesus from the dead? God. What was that moment like, exactly? Hard to say—have you ever noticed that the Gospels don't actually tell us that part of the story?

Hebrews holds tightly to the full humanity and the full deity of Jesus. He created everything, he sustains everything, he is the "radiance of God's glory and the exact representation of his being" (Heb 1:1-4). In Hebrews 1:8, the Father even calls the Son "God"! And, of course, it says that he was made exactly like us (Heb 2:17). It also says that he had to be one of us in order to be our priest (Heb 5:1), which means he had to be fully human in order to accomplish atonement.

Further Resources

Bettenson, Henry, and Chris Maunder, eds. *Documents of the Christian Church*. 3rd ed. Oxford: Oxford University Press, 1999.

Brennan, Nick. *Divine Christology in the Epistle to the Hebrews: The Son as God*. Library of New Testament Studies 656. London: T&T Clark, 2021.

Crisp, Oliver D. "Desiderata for Models of the Hypostatic Union." In *Christology Ancient and Modern: Explorations in Constructive Dogmatics*, edited by Oliver D. Crisp and Fred Sanders, 19-41. Grand Rapids, MI: Zondervan, 2013.

Greer, Rowan A. *The Captain of Our Salvation: A Study in the Patristic Exegesis of Hebrews*. Beitrage zur Geschichte der Biblischen Exegese 15. Tübingen: Mohr Siebeck, 1973.

Kibbe, Michael H. "'You Are a Priest Forever!' Jesus' Indestructible Life in Hebrews 7:16." *Horizons in Biblical Theology* 39 (2017): 134-55.

Webster, John B. "One Who Is Son: Theological Reflections on the Exordium to the Epistle to the Hebrews." In *The Epistle to the Hebrews and Christian Theology*, edited by Richard Bauckham, Daniel R. Driver, Trevor A. Hart, and Nathan MacDonald, 69-94. Grand Rapids, MI: Eerdmans, 2009.

Yeago, David S. "The New Testament and the Nicene Dogma: A Contribution to the Recovery of Theological Exegesis." *Pro Ecclesia* 3 (1994): 152-64.

THE ASCENSION

YEAR AFTER YEAR, I ASK MY STUDENTS whether they've ever heard a sermon on the ascension. Read a book on the ascension. Heard a podcast on the ascension. Given the ascension any focused attention whatsoever. And year after year, it's the same response: no, no, no, and no. And yet consider these words attributed to Saint Augustine:

> The festival of the ascension "is that festival which confirms the grace of all the festivals together, without which the profitableness of every festival would have perished. For unless the Savior had ascended into heaven, His Nativity would have come to nothing . . . and His Passion would have borne no fruit for us, and His most Holy Resurrection would have been useless."[1]

Imagine that: a moment in the story of Jesus without which his birth, death, and resurrection would have been a waste of time—and we never talk about it. Why is that? I can think of a few reasons. First, we don't read the creeds—or our own doctrinal statements, for that matter. There's no creed or confession or doctrinal statement in the history of the Christian church that doesn't include the ascension as the true and necessary event that took place after Jesus' resurrection and before Pentecost. When we ignore the ascension, we are out of step with what the church has always believed.

Second, we think the important events are the ones that happen on earth—like earth is the stage, and heaven is the wings, the sound booth, something like that. But that's not how the Bible tells the story. Things

---

[1]As cited in J. G. Davies, *He Ascended into Heaven: A Study in the History of Doctrine* (New York: Association Press, 1958), 170.

happen in heaven. Imagine trying to understand Job without the first part of the story where God and Satan have their debates about Job's faithfulness. Or how about Revelation? John is taken up into heaven (Rev 4:1-2) so he can see clearly the events in heaven and their import for subsequent events on earth.

Here's why this point matters for the ascension. A third (but related to the second) reason we ignore the ascension is that we think the Bible just doesn't say much. Luke 24:51—Jesus was carried up into heaven. Acts 1:9—Jesus was lifted up and hidden by a cloud. And that's it. That's the whole story of the ascension as narrated by the Gospels. Not much, right? How could that possibly be as important as his death and resurrection? But those two verses are telling the story of the ascension from an earthly perspective. And from an earthly perspective, it's very simple: Jesus *left*. But what about the ascension from a heavenly perspective?

According to Hebrews 1, the ascension from a heavenly perspective means not Jesus *leaving* but Jesus *coming*. He *arrives*, and he is welcomed by his Father as the Lord of all creation and enthroned above the angels. And according to Hebrews 9, Jesus arrived in heaven and, before sitting down, completed his work of atonement by presenting himself to his Father, and in doing so purified us to enter heaven and even purified heaven itself. Atonement and enthronement: both functions of the ascension, according to Hebrews. We're not going to get any of that from the Gospels, because that's not their angle. We need Hebrews (mostly by way of quoting a bunch of psalms) to tell us that part of the story.

The last reason we don't pay attention to the ascension is that we tend to think, even if subconsciously, that the ascension is when Jesus finally quit being human and went back to being God. But that doesn't work on multiple fronts. First, because Jesus didn't quit being God when he became human. And second, because he didn't quit being human when he ascended. What would the point of the resurrection have been if Jesus were going to shuck that new-creation body as soon as he was hidden in the clouds? He is and was and has always been God. At a point in time, he became human, and remains so to this day.

So what happened in the ascension, and why does it matter? Jesus, the eternal Son, the God-man, the Word-made-flesh, arrived in heaven, the first resurrected human to be with God in the fullest possible sense and the only human to reign over the works of God's hands as we were intended to do. But he didn't do this just for his own benefit but for ours: so that we might be fully present with God and that we might also rule over the "world to come," as Hebrews 2:5 calls it. Without the ascension, we have neither full access to God our Father nor full restoration of our place in his world. The future of redeemed humanity of course needs the birth, death, and resurrection of Jesus—but without the ascension, the prodigal children could never truly come home.

Further Resources

Chester, Tim, and Jonny Woodrow. *The Ascension: Humanity in the Presence of God*. Ross-shire, UK: Christian Focus, 2013.

Davies, J. G. *He Ascended into Heaven: A Study in the History of Doctrine*. New York: Association, 1958.

Farrow, Douglas. *Ascension and Ecclesia: On the Significance of the Doctrine of the Ascension for Ecclesiology and Christian Cosmology*. Edinburgh: T&T Clark, 1999.

———. *Ascension Theology*. London: T&T Clark, 2011.

McIlroy, David H. "Toward a Relational and Trinitarian Theology of Atonement." *Evangelical Quarterly* 80 (2008): 13-32.

Orr, Peter C. *Exalted Above the Heavens: The Risen and Ascended Christ*. New Studies in Biblical Theology. Downers Grove, IL: IVP Academic, 2018.

Schreiner, Patrick. *The Ascension of Christ: Recovering a Neglected Doctrine*. Snapshots. Bellingham, WA: Lexham, 2020.

THE ATONEMENT

ATONEMENT. ALL THAT GOD HAS DONE for us in Christ. The scholarly conversation frequently revolves around the relative usefulness of four models for the atonement: penal substitution, *Christus Victor*, recapitulation, and moral influence. Recapitulation has to do with Jesus as a second Adam—the embodiment of humanity restored to its original image-bearing form and function. Penal substitution means Jesus took the penalty of our sin. *Christus Victor* implies that Jesus conquered Sin and Death and all manner of evil powers in his death, resurrection, and ascension. And moral influence means that he gave us an example of how to live and made it possible for us to follow that example.

Some people debate which one of these four is right, to the exclusion of the others. Others argue that all four are correct, in various ways and in various texts. And still others argue not only that all four are biblical but that there are biblical ways of thinking about how they relate to one another. I'll specifically commend to you Joshua McNall's book *The Mosaic of the Atonement*, in which he depicts a four-piece mosaic, the fullness of which images Christ in cruciform stance, and names recapitulation as the feet, penal substitution as the heart, *Christus Victor* as the head, and moral influence as the hands. You ought to read his book, but here's the quick recap: Because the Son is the original image of the Father from which humanity was formed, it is appropriate that the Son actually become human, thereby relocating humanity from being "in Adam" to being "in Christ" (recapitulation). Because he is the true head of humanity, he is qualified to receive God's just punishment in our place, instead of us (penal substitution). By doing that, there no longer is any accusation that Satan might bring against us, no longer any claim

that Death might make over us (*Christus Victor*). And we live into that
new reality as the Holy Spirit both beckons us into living as Christ did
and restrains us from falling back into our old enslaved life (moral influence)—thus, we are conformed into his image, completing the circle
back into recapitulation.

One element of atonement not encapsulated in this mosaic is the
redemption of all things—the new creation itself. Hebrews speaks to our
salvation, which is the inheritance of the world to come, wherein everything is put back in order and under our feet (Heb 2:5-10). Paul makes
a similar point in different terms when he says that creation is longing
for the children of God to be revealed (Rom 8:19). Why is it longing for
this? "Because creation has been subjected to futility, not willingly, but
because of the one who subjected it in expectation that creation itself
will be set free from slavery to corruption and brought into the glorious
freedom of God's children" (Rom 8:20-21). In other words: *our* redemption is the prerequisite for *creation's* redemption, because creation
finds its proper place in God's economy only when we find ours.

The entire process of atonement is accomplished by the mysterious
reality that theologians call union with Christ. Because the Holy
Spirit has put us in Christ, we receive *his* life, *his* relationship with the
Father, *his* status in the world. Even though we are still, practically
speaking, constantly disintegrating ourselves, he holds us together.
Even when we die (theologically speaking, death is when our souls
and bodies are separated) and are compositionally disintegrated, we
remain in Christ and so find in him the promise of resurrection.
Perhaps the most immediately practical point to be made here is that
we are prone to prioritizing the gifts over the Giver. We have an abun-
dance of blessings in Christ: redemption, justification, reconciliation,
salvation, sanctification, eternal life, and so on. But those are not
handouts; they are not objects passed from Christ to us, as though we
could have them apart from him. We have them *in him* and only *in
him*. Union with Christ is the one fundamental salvific good, and
everything else comes as a result.

Further Resources

Baker, Mark D., and Joel B. Green. *Recovering the Scandal of the Cross*. 2nd ed. Downers Grove, IL: InterVarsity Press, 2011.

Billings, J. Todd. *Union with Christ: Reframing Theology and Ministry for the Church*. Grand Rapids, MI: Baker Academic, 2011.

Campbell, Constantine R. *Paul and Union with Christ: An Exegetical and Theological Study*. Grand Rapids, MI: Zondervan, 2012.

Crisp, Oliver D., and Fred Sanders, eds. *Locating Atonement: Explorations in Constructive Dogmatics*. Grand Rapids, MI: Zondervan, 2015.

Macaskill, Grant. *Union with Christ in the New Testament*. Oxford: Oxford University Press, 2013.

McNall, Joshua M. *The Mosaic of the Atonement: An Integrated Approach to Christ's Work*. Grand Rapids, MI: Zondervan, 2019.

Thate, Michael J., Kevin J. Vanhoozer, and Constantine R. Campbell, eds. *"In Christ" in Paul: Explorations in Paul's Theology of Union and Participation*. Grand Rapids, MI: Eerdmans, 2018.

Treat, Jeremy. *The Crucified King: Atonement and Kingdom in Biblical and Systematic Theology*. Grand Rapids, MI: Zondervan, 2014.

SCRIPTURE INDEX